Write Better Multiple-Choice Questions to Assess Learning

Measure What Matters—
Evidence-Informed Tactics for
Multiple-Choice Questions

Patti Shank, PhD

Patti Shank PhD/Learning Peaks LLC
www.pattishank.com

Write Better Multiple-Choice Questions to Assess Learning—1st ed.
ISBN: 9798453383993

Praise for *Write Better Multiple-Choice Questions*

When I want an easily comprehensible way to create tests and, specifically, multiple choice questions, I go to Patti Shank. She has succinctly offered her question creation wisdom in an uber-useful book, *Write Better Multiple-Choice Questions*. There are a few great books I like to give to clients and colleagues. This is now among those. Thanks, Patti, for filling a much-needed void.
Matthew Richter
President of the Thiagi Group, Facilitator, Game Designer, Instructional Designer, And Management Consultant

Patti Shank has become known as a reliable resource for carefully researched, thoughtfully documented advice on key instructional design challenges. This latest addition to Patti's series of guidebooks is yet another example of everything we've come to expect from her. Patti has filled this book with practical step-by-step guidance, useful examples and thought-provoking tools to help readers better understand multiple-choice logic and improve their ability to put that logic to work in the real world.
John Leh
CEO, Lead Analyst, Talented Learning

This book will become a "must-have" for anyone writing learning activities. It helps instructional designers, trainers, and anyone responsible for creating usable training, craft relevant activities, and post-course assessments. Armed with the tactics in the book, readers can create assessments that genuinely test someone's ability to perform a task or apply knowledge to a job context. I think it's a hugely valuable addition to the field of L&D/T&D. Thank you for putting it together.
Sharon Boller
Author and Speaker, Affiliate Consultant for Tier1 Performance

I found what I was looking for in this book. My first language is not English, so the easy-to-understand writing and advice was very helpful. The full bibliography was extremely valuable.
Aude Caussarieu
Didactic Sciences

In the L&D industry, there are several dozen important authors you should be reading. Patti is even rarer. She combines practical application with research-supported content. She is a stellar example of the singular handful of individuals in this category. Anything she writes should not only be on your to-read list. It must be on your to-read-right-now list. *Write Better Multiple-Choice Questions* is another worthy addition to the must-read and must-reference-often list.

Bill Sawyer
Oracle Corporation

I now understand the science behind writing these questions and a clear process to follow—one that starts at the beginning with identifying what needs to be learned and what needs to be demonstrated. One of the key benefits for me is now being able to offer constructive suggestions to those writing multiple-choice questions that will add value to their work.

Kath Cherrie
National Vice President, New Zealand Association for Training and Development

Multiple-choice questions are one of the most readily available tools for people who design learning experiences, and MCQs are one of the most frequently misused learning tools. Patti has created the best resource on the when, why, and how of creating effective multiple-choice questions.

Julie Dirksen
Author of *Design for How People Learn*

This is a very worthy addition to the library of every instructional developer, designer, and even every analyst. Patti provides much more than just how to create valid multiple-choice questions and does so in an easy-to-read and very actionable manner.

Guy W. Wallace
President, EPPIC Inc.

Patti Shank does it again! By doing exhaustive research and translating it with a practitioner's wisdom, Patti gives us clear, energizing, and practical advice so we can create powerfully effective multiple-choice questions on our own!

Will Thalheimer
Author, *Performance-Focused Smile Sheets*, Work-Learning Research, Inc.

THANK YOU.

I had a lot of help getting this book from course manual to book. I need to thank...

My husband Steve. When I feel like I can't, he reminds me that I can.

Sharon Boller, author of *Design Thinking for Training and Development: Creating Learning Journeys That Get Results*, offered critical guidance on the manuscript. Her input improved the book. Her introduction to the book offers important insights about assessments and multiple-choice questions.

The following colleagues reviewed earlier versions of the book and offered enormously helpful feedback.
Saul Carliner
Aude Caussarieu
Kath Cherrie
Jeff Dalto
Julie Dirksen
Prakhar Jain
John Leh
Felix Nater
Clark Quinn
Matthew Richter
Bill Sawyer
Fernando Senior
Will Thalheimer
Guy Wallace
Julie Yamamoto

My editors:
Ann Battenfield
Ross Edwards

Course participants asked great questions, which pushed me to find and interpret research. Some of them reviewed this book. The community of multiple-choice question geeks continues to grow!

Readers are the most important reason for writing. I'm indebted to you.

Contents

Sharon's Introduction

The reality TV show *The Great British Baking Show* is wildly popular. It's essentially a performance assessment for master bakers. The intrigue centers on a group of people who prove their skills via a series of challenges. The challenges are a comprehensive assessment of contestants' technical, creative, and time management skills. If you make it to the finals on *The Great British Baking Show,* you KNOW you are a stellar baker. So do all the viewers and other bakers who are part of the show. Your ability to produce one delectable baked good after another is ample evidence of your master baker status.

After I read Patti Shank's wonderful new book, I thought about *The Great British Baking Show* and its huge fan base. Clearly, many of us enjoy seeing people challenged to demonstrate competence. We also value assessments as consumers. We want evidence of competence in the form of certifications or licensing (accountants, lawyers, physicians, teachers, fitness trainers, therapists, and more.) We want evidence of quality and competent operations when we select restaurants, lawn services, hair stylists, hotels, or cars. Star ratings, coupled with reviewers' feedback, help us feel confidence in the competence of the people providing the experiences we buy.

The right assessments similarly:

- Help learners verify they understand what's being taught as they complete a course.
- Help course developers verify that learners learn what the developer intends them to learn.
- Help assess learner competence and ability to apply knowledge or perform a skill after they complete a course.
- Let people reflect on their own learning, which helps them retain the learning.

In short, well-crafted assessments provide evidence that someone does or doesn't know something or can or cannot do something. And that evidence indicates whether a company has generated a good return on its investment in a training or education solution.

Conversely, badly designed and poorly constructed assessments waste time and money. Joining them in the money-wasting department are courses that dump content on learners without any in-course or post-course assessment. High-quality assessment helps us measure what matters.

Patti Shank comes to the rescue with this book. I've been a Patti Shank fan for a long time as she delivers consistently practical advice on how to apply learning science research in the practice of creating learning. She does exactly that with this book—delivering clear, research-based explanations and practical step-by-step guidance.

The book does two things. First, it provides an overall primer on assessments and the terminology you need to understand, such as validity and reliability. Second, it gives readers a practical "how-to" guide to create the most common assessment item: multiple-choice questions.

Patti guides us in how to avoid common mistakes of poor assessment design and poor multiple-choice item construction. Her explanations, examples, and exercises work together to build readers' knowledge and skill. In other words, Patti tells AND shows. This blend of explanation, example, and practice makes the book valuable for both novice content developers and seasoned L&D professionals. Why? Because few of us, unless we are trained psychometricians, have expertise crafting quality assessments.

In education and training, organizations waste a ton of money creating content called "training" or "courses" that don't end up teaching anyone anything. If organizations are going to spend money developing training, those same organizations should care about assessing whether people acquired knowledge or skills from that training.

Patti's book provides the roadmap to how to accomplish this goal in a realistic way. Best of all, from my perspective, it's a book I can return to again and again for "just-in-time" guidance to help me design and write good assessments or help me coach clients who edit or rewrite well-crafted assessment items and make them...well...NOT well crafted.

Sharon Boller
Author and Speaker, Affiliate Consultant for TiER1 Performance

Saul's Introduction

Years ago, I heard an adult educator advise novice instructional designers to write multiple-choice questions solely to engage learners. That would be fine if that were the only purpose. Multiple-choice questions are ultimately used in training to assess the likelihood that participants can perform on the job. That has implications for those who depend on these people to complete work responsibilities and, just as importantly, to the participants' careers. In other words, despite their seeming simplicity, writing effective and meaningful multiple-choice (and other forms of objective questions that effectively assess learning) involves myriad considerations.

No one presents those considerations in as clear and usable way as Patti Shank. That's not surprising, given her other books that translate learning science into guidance that practicing professionals can use.

This book covers key considerations in writing effective multiple-choice questions, including choosing question formats; constructing effective questions; choosing an appropriate number of questions; using multiple-choice questions to assess higher-order skills; providing feedback; and scoring.

To do so in a relevant way, Shank provides insights from practice, examples, and summaries called "insights" in each chapter. She does not sacrifice rigor in doing so; the reference lists in each chapter include classics, authoritative references, and contemporary references on issues related to writing multiple-choice and other forms of objective questions.

Saul Carliner
Professor of Educational Technology, Concordia University, Montreal

Why I Wrote This Book

Why would an instructional designer write a book on multiple-choice questions? There are already excellent and authoritative books on assessment and multiple-choice questions written by educational measurement experts. I have most of them.

It's not that there aren't good books on this topic. The problem is the excellent and authoritative books written by educational measurement experts can be difficult to read. Many don't discuss basics in easy-to-understand, practical ways.

I didn't set out to write a book but to help people who needed to write good multiple-choice questions. This book started as notes and has grown over many years. I also didn't start out to teach these skills but, as I read and applied the research, I wanted to help others apply it, too.

The book is for anyone who designs training for adults, whether they have a training or instructional title or not. This includes instructional designers, trainers, and instructors, of course. But it also includes human resource, sales, technology, and safety folks as well as experts, health educators, and volunteer coordinators—anyone who must train others and assess their learning. Everyone who uses multiple-choice questions must be able to write them so participants aren't frustrated and can show what they have learned.

This book isn't meant to replace the authoritative books written by educational measurement experts. Rather, it's meant for everyday workplace and adult learning practitioners and experts who need to do a better job with multiple-choice questions that assess learning. It's straightforward and pragmatic.

My focus in this book is narrow: **Writing performance-based learning objectives and multiple-choice questions to assess them**. I include additional information I believe will help you understand the bigger picture, but the additional information is not meant to be comprehensive. Writing performance-based learning objectives and multiple-choice questions to assess them is an important, worthwhile, and challenging skill by itself.

Patti Shank
Digital Learning and Learning Sciences Author and Facilitator

Chapter 1:
What Are We Doing?

Léo works in contract management and helps others use the contract management application. He recently got a call from legal about contract omissions and inaccuracies. Lily works directly with customers who use her company's cloud-based integrated application. Leaders want to certify people to reduce problems that occur when people don't use the application properly. Leilani created a unique stretching method based on body mechanics research and wants to make sure her instructors know how to appropriately teach her method.

Léo, Lilly, and Leilani have similar concerns, even though they have very different jobs. All of them have a critical and important need to make sure people can perform as needed and achieve needed results. Each needs to identify what people must be able to do. And they need a way to determine whether those results are achieved.

If your work involves helping people perform, it is critical for you, too, to identify the required skills and determine if needed results are achieved. The process described in this book is meant to help Léo, Lilly, Leilani, and *you* to create effective multiple-choice questions (Chapters 3-7) that assess whether participants have achieved what they need to learn (Chapter 2).

Why Multiple-Choice

People use multiple-choice questions because they're efficient to deliver and score. Well-written multiple-choice questions allow us to:
- Efficiently measure a wide range of knowledge and skills,
- Easily and objectively score assessments,
- Assess understanding and use of knowledge and skills, and
- Reduce costs and time for assessment (Gierl et al., 2017).

To be valid, assessments must assess a representative sample of knowledge and skills from the area tested. Assessing a representative sample of knowledge and skills can be time consuming. The efficiency of multiple-choice questions makes this possible (Haladyna, 1997).

Multiple-choice questions can't adequately assess all learning objectives, so I include information about performance assessments in this chapter. Still, multiple-choice questions are regarded as one of the most widely applicable testing methods.

Multiple-Choice Challenges

While delivering and scoring multiple-choice questions is *efficient*, there are some challenges to overcome to also make them *effective*. I'll describe two main challenges we need to overcome to create effective multiple-choice assessments.

Challenge 1. There are so many ways to write bad questions.

Consider the poorly-written multiple-choice question below. How many problems can you find?

What is the correct way to rotate fresh produce in the produce department? (Select the correct answer.)
  a) Lift the display and rotate it 90 degrees.
  b) Swap fruit or vegetables from one end of the store to the other end.
  c) Move the oldest produce to the top of the display and add fresher produce from stock to the bottom of the display.
  d) None of the above.

This question has serious problems! The incorrect answers a and b are not plausible, making it easy to eliminate them as the correct answer. Answer c is the longest and has the most depth, which is an obvious clue that it is the correct answer. The last answer choice, d, is an answer choice we shouldn't use (discussed in Chapter 3). People often make these mistakes, as well as others.

Guessing the correct answer when the question is poorly written is often easy, as seen in the example. This is *absolutely not what we want*.

Consider this "fixed" example, created with the evidence-informed writing guidelines described in this book.

What is the correct way to rotate fresh produce in the produce department? (Select the correct answer.)
   a)   Discard older produce and restock with fresh produce from stock.
   b)   Restock fresh produce and then stack good older product on top.
   c)   Put older produce on sales racks and restock with fresh produce.

In this rewrite, all incorrect answers are plausible. There are no clues as to the correct answer. I removed "None of the above" as an answer choice. It is no longer easy to guess the correct answer. And it has three answer choices, because research shows this is often the best number of answer choices (discussed in Chapter 3).

Challenge 2. There's a lot to know to write effective multiple-choice questions.

Writing good multiple-choice questions involves some challenging skills. They include:
   • Writing good learning objectives so we know what to assess with our questions.
   • Writing multiple-choice questions that assess important knowledge and skills in the learning objectives so assessments measure the right things.
   • Following evidence-informed question writing guidelines, which make questions easier to understand and harder to guess, so information gained from assessments is accurate and valuable.

Using these skills to write good questions prevents a host of problems, including morale problems from confusing or unfair assessments, unusable assessment results, and legal problems due to unfair and invalid assessments. And we cannot forget the credibility damage caused by poorly-written assessments.

While it takes effort to learn to write good multiple-choice questions, it is certainly worth the effort considering the problems prevented. Like most skills, we get better over time with practice, so this challenge becomes easier.

One of my clients develops technical training; their question writers are content experts. When we started working together, I wrote their questions and we edited them together. After three weeks they could write decent questions that I edited to better follow evidence-based guidelines. After a few more weeks, their questions required few edits. Now? They check in from time to time.

What Should We Assess?

Assessment means measuring learning outcomes to find out whether needed outcomes were achieved. My colleague, Will Thalheimer (2018), created the *Learning Transfer Evaluation Model* (LTEM) in response to the shortcomings he saw in the Kirkpatrick model (1959). Below is a concise overview of the model.

	Tier	Description
8	Effects of Transfer	Instructional outcomes which affect learners, coworkers/family/friends, the organization, the community, society, and the environs.
7	Transfer	Learner uses what was learned to perform work tasks successfully, as demonstrated through objective measures.
6	Task Competence	Learner performs relevant realistic actions and decision making.
5	Decision Making Competence	Learner makes decisions given relevant realistic scenarios.
4	Knowledge	Learner answers questions about facts/terminology.
3	Learner Perceptions	Learner answers questions about course satisfaction, course reputation, etc.
2	Activity	Learner engages in learning activities.
1	Attendance	Learner signs up, starts, attends, or completes a learning experience.

LTEM Model, used with Will Thalheimer's permission, https://www.worklearning.com

Because it often is difficult to assess what we really want to know (Tiers 7 and 8), we settle for proxies. Proxies are stand-ins for something or someone else. For example, someone named to make healthcare decisions for you when you cannot do so is acting as your proxy.

Many learning practitioners and instructors construe attendance or completing activities (Tiers 1 and 2) as proxies for achieving needed outcomes. The problem is they aren't good proxies. People easily attend and engage in activities without achieving needed learning outcomes.

To assess whether people can do what we teach them, we must aim higher. Tiers 5 and 6 on the LTEM chart are what we should primarily assess with multiple-choice questions.

Research is clear that well-written multiple-choice questions can measure a wide range of important learning outcomes, including analysis, decision making, and problem solving (Haladyna, 1997, 2004). Fortunately, research also shows that well-written, higher-level multiple-choice assessments can be an effective proxy for higher levels of measurement (Drake Prometric, 1995).

Why Assessment Matters

There are many reasons to assess learning. The primary reason discussed in this book is to find out whether participants achieved needed learning outcomes. Assessment also supplies critical information we need to improve instruction.

Those who train others may mistakenly believe the needed outcome is that the content they created is used. The use of content is not our primary job, however. Our primary job is to facilitate needed knowledge and skills and needed outcomes. When we don't build needed knowledge and skills, the needed outcomes are not likely met, and our work is far less valuable.

To build needed knowledge and skills, we need to analyze whether our instruction, as created, builds the skills it is supposed to build. That's what this book is about: to analyze the skills people need, and then to write multiple-choice questions to see if participants achieved those skills.

There are other benefits of good assessments, including memory gains. Because this book deals primarily with summative assessment, the focus is on written assessments to assess whether the desired learning objectives were achieved. Performance assessments and formative assessments are briefly discussed.

Formative and Summative Assessment

Formative (during instruction) and summative (after instruction) assessments help us analyze whether participants are gaining or have gained the needed knowledge and skills.

Formative assessment includes activities that occur during instruction. It identifies the misunderstandings and missing understandings participants have so we can fix them while instruction is in progress. Examples of common formative assessments include open questions, quiz questions, and activities.

For example, a course for people newly diagnosed with diabetes might use formative assessment to determine whether participants know the symptoms of low and high blood sugar. The following image shows what this kind of formative assessment activity might look like.

Symptoms of low and high blood sugar

Instructions: Sort each symptom by dragging it into one of two categories: *Symptom of low blood sugar* or *Symptom of high blood sugar*. You will see if your answer is correct while you sort.

Sweating

Symptom of low blood sugar   Symptom of high blood sugar

Based on the results, the course could offer feedback, suggest additional content, or progress to new content.

Formative assessment informs next steps by designers, instructors, and participants (Black & Wiliam, 2007). The primary goal is to examine what participants struggle with and what does not work well, then to fix those issues.

Summative assessment evaluates achievement of the learning objectives—typically at the end of an instructional unit. Some examples of common summative assessments are tests, simulations, and skill demonstrations.

For example, a course for people newly diagnosed with diabetes might have a summative assessment at the end of each module. The module on analyzing blood sugar results might include the following multiple-choice question.

Question 5 of 15

Two hours after eating lunch, you check your blood sugar. The reading: 384 mg/dL. This reading indicates that your blood sugar is: (Select the correct answer.)

○ Too low
○ Normal
○ Too high

Summative assessments should help designers and instructors understand the degree to which instruction helped participants meet the learning objectives, which helps continuously improve instruction.

It may have occurred to you that we could have switched the formative and summative assessment examples. We could use the sorting exercise for summative assessment and the multiple-choice question for formative assessment. It's not the activity type so much as the intention and use of the results that makes an assessment formative or summative.

This book concentrates on multiple-choice questions used in summative assessments. It will also help you with multiple-choice questions used for formative assessments.

There often isn't a clear line between formative assessment and summative assessment. The quiz at the end of each of my course modules is summative in that it's at the end of each module. The primary purpose is to help course participants analyze whether they understood the module's critical points. These quizzes serve many of the purposes of formative *and* summative assessment.

Formative assessment and summative assessment are part of the same process: to identify what participants gained from instruction. Formative assessment helps us make needed course corrections. We can then measure the effectiveness of instructional activities and course corrections with summative assessment. The following image shows how I think of the process.

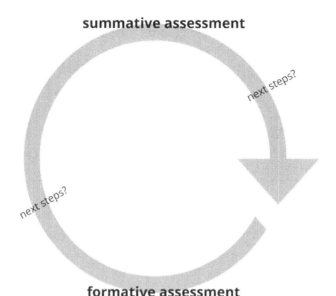

Ideally, formative assessment surfaces and helps us fix problems, but summative assessment may find more. Should we leave people with misunderstandings and missing understandings because the module or course is over? I think it's obvious that we shouldn't—especially with important knowledge and skills.

Mastery learning is an instructional approach that intentionally combines formative and summative assessment. In it, participants are expected to achieve the learning objectives before moving to the next unit. When mastery isn't achieved, assessments are formative in nature and participants access support needed to achieve mastery. When mastery is achieved, assessments are summative in nature and participants move on.

When to (Optimally) Write Assessments

The following diagram shows the process for building relevant assessments. Tasks that are covered in depth in this book are in darker boxes with light text. I briefly discuss the other tasks to help you understand the bigger picture.

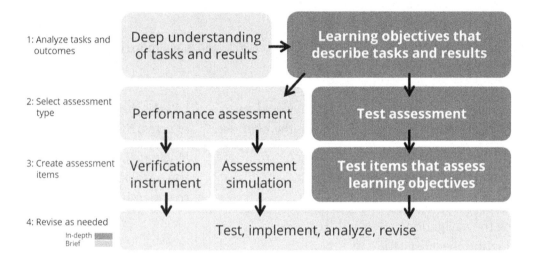

Items=Test questions or activities

Designing assessments appropriately occurs early during design—right after identifying learning objectives. Assessments must align with objectives, and this helps ensure you assess what's needed.

When we wait until later to develop assessments (a common but unfortunate mistake), other parts of the design process will influence the assessments—and assessments are less likely to be meaningful or appropriate.

If you find it difficult to write assessment items, that's a clue the objective is problematic. Chapter 2 will help you build good learning objectives.

TRY THIS!

Exercise 1-1. Does each learning objective below make it obvious how to assess? What is the obvious way to assess the learning objective?

I completed the first item to show you how to do the exercise.

Exercise answers are at the end of this chapter. You will learn more if you do the exercise *before* you review the answers.

Learning objective	Is it obvious how to assess this objective?	What is the obvious way to assess this objective?
Understand the best navigation scheme for a website.	Yes **No**	Unclear. What exactly is the participant supposed to show she can do?
Using the navigation evaluation checklist, students will find three websites with good navigation design.	Yes No	
If a situation allows for time off, the supervisor will analyze whether it qualifies for paid or unpaid time off.	Yes No	

Valid Assessments

You often hear the term "validity" when assessments are discussed. That's because a valid assessment measures what it claims to measure. An assessment of the ability to complete a specific task should measure the degree to which the task is completed according to specified criteria.

The graphic below is a simple metaphor for a valid assessment. The center of the target represents the learning objective. The arrow hitting the center represents the assessment measuring the learning objective. This indicates a valid assessment.

Validity is a matter of degree rather than an absolute. In addition, an assessment may be valid for some purposes and not others, so it is far less useful to say an assessment is valid than to say an assessment is valid for a specific purpose.

Reliability means the assessment works consistently. If you get on a bathroom scale three times in a row and the weight on the scale is different each time, the scale measures inconsistently and is therefore not reliable. No matter why it is inconsistent, you cannot have confidence in the results.

The next image shows the same metaphor. We see a consistent result because all arrows hit the same place. But they didn't land in the center, so while the result is reliable, it isn't valid.

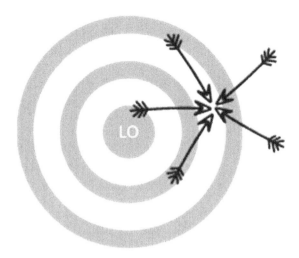

If an assessment is unreliable, it cannot be valid—because unreliable scores do not consistently measure what we intend them to measure. Unreliable assessments are not valid.

The image below shows the metaphor once again. We see that the assessment measures consistently and it measures the learning objectives. It is both valid and reliable.

We are interested primarily in validity. We consider reliability because an assessment can't be valid if isn't reliable. A valid assessment, on the other hand, assures a certain degree of reliability. There are some common tactics that make course-based assessments more valid and reliable.

For more valid assessments:
- Make sure there is alignment between objectives and assessment items.
- Have multiple content experts and proficient practitioners review items to confirm they measure the right knowledge and skills.
- Create a larger percentage of assessment items for the most critical objectives.
- Verify that assessment items are relevant and not trivial.
- Make items as hard (or easy) as the task they measure.

For more reliable assessments:
- Reduce guessing by eliminating item flaws that increase guessing.
- Make sure items are clearly written, written at the right level, and unambiguous.
- Have enough items to cover all objectives adequately. Ideally, assess each objective with multiple items—especially for important objectives.
- Provide checklists or rubrics to evaluate performance or essay-type answers.
- Remove as many barriers that impact test performance as possible.

I describe three assessment situations below. One is neither valid nor reliable. One is valid and reliable. One is reliable but not valid. Can you figure out which is which?
- You want to assess authoring skills, so you ask test takers to run one mile in as little time as possible.
- You want to assess completion of a document, but the instructions are quite hard to understand.
- You want to assess ability to identify the meaning of medical terms, so you ask test takers to identify the meaning of a variety of medical terms.

If you want to measure authoring skills, you must measure authoring skills according to provided standards. If you instead measure how fast participants can run one mile, you are likely to have a reliable but invalid assessment. It's reliable because test takers will likely run the mile in a similar amount of time each time they try, but it measures running rather than authoring. This assessment situation is reliable but not valid.

If you want to measure ability to complete a document, you should measure completion of the document according to provided standards. But, if the instructions are hard to understand, you are likely to have an unreliable assessment. It's unreliable because only those who understand it are likely to do it correctly. It is invalid because it is likely to measure comprehension of the instructions more than completion of the document. This assessment situation is neither reliable nor valid.

If you want to measure the ability to identify the meaning of medical terms, you should measure whether test takers can identify the meaning of medical terms. It's valid because it measures the right thing. If the assessment is written clearly and understandably, items measure what was taught, and there aren't any barriers to taking the assessment, it is likely to be reliable. This assessment situation is valid and reliable.

TRY THIS!

Exercise 1-2. Which of the following proposed changes to an assessment will improve validity? Which will improve reliability?

I completed the first item to show you how to do the exercise.

Exercise answers are at the end of this chapter. You will learn more if you do the exercise before you review the answers.

Proposed change	Improve validity?	Improve reliability?
Write clearly written questions.		✓
Make sure the items measure attainment of the objectives.		
Increase the number of items for the most important objectives.		
Improve wording clarity so items are easier to understand.		

How problematic is it when we don't build optimal assessments? It depends on the stakes (consequences) of the assessment. When certifying that a learner has specific skills—and these skills are critical (for example, packing parachutes or handling hazardous materials)—it is critical to ensure the assessments are valid and reliable. If the assessment affects a person's livelihood, assessments must be as valid and reliable as possible.

MORE...

If you need more guidance on validity, here are two excellent books:

Shrock, S. A. & Coscarelli, W. C. (2007). Criterion-referenced test development: Technical and legal guidelines for corporate training. Hoboken: John Wiley & Sons.

Haladyna, T. M. & Rodriguez, M. (2013). Developing and validating test items. New York, NY: Routledge, Taylor and Francis Group.

I also recommend these two articles from NCZER Press:
A hitchhiker's guide to reliability
A hitchhiker's guide to validity

To maintain the URLs more easily for online resources, they are available here: https://www.pattishank.com/mcqresources

Criterion-Referenced Assessments

Criterion-referenced assessments assess participants against specific criteria— the learning objectives. When we write good questions and they align with the learning objectives, we confirm that participants have met the criteria (Shrock & Coscarelli, 2007).

Recall that the purpose of summative assessment is to confirm or certify specific knowledge and skills. These assessments are a substitute for directly observing people doing the job over time. We use this substitution because direct observation is time consuming, expensive, and rarely occurs. When we write good assessments, they are suitable proxies for direct observation (Drake Prometric, 1995).

Developing tests that are valid and reliable requires objectives that accurately reflect job knowledge and skills and assessments that accurately measure achievement of the objectives. As a result, objectives must describe essential knowledge and skills and test items must measure whether participants can demonstrate essential knowledge and skills.

Performance vs. Test Assessments

There are two main formats for criterion-referenced assessments: Performance assessments and test assessments. Although both are "tests" of sorts, performance assessments assess performance in a more realistic way while test assessments use paper- or computer-based multiple-choice, matching, and short- and long-answer (i.e., essay) type questions.

The optimal assessment format depends on whether the objective is declarative (list, match, define …) or procedural (calculate, analyze, decide…). Research shows there is a big difference between these two types of knowledge. Declarative knowledge is knowing about while procedural knowledge is knowing how.

When I travel, I often read information in advance about how to get around. Before leaving, I usually have an idea how to use the subway and how to get to the places I want to visit. This is declarative knowledge. While visiting and using the subway system to buy tickets, find my stops, and transfer to other subway lines, I am using procedural knowledge.

We typically want to assess procedural knowledge. Why? We want to assess what participants can *do*, not just what they *know*. Many people don't think we can assess procedural knowledge with multiple-choice questions. As a result, they may assess only declarative knowledge such as terminology or other facts. Or they may not test because they think multiple-choice testing is deficient. But multiple-choice questions can and should be written to assess procedural knowledge because these are the types of questions that are reasonable proxies for assessing what people can do.

Performance Assessments

Performance assessments are optimal for procedural objectives and typically aim to test learners in real or realistic situations to assess complex knowledge and skills. Two of the most commonly used tools for performance assessments are verification instruments (real-world) and assessment simulations or scenarios (simulated real-world or descriptions of real-world situations).

My multiple-choice writing course and this book concentrate on multiple-choice questions. Because we can't assess all objectives with multiple-choice questions, I want you to see checklists, rating scales, and assessment scenarios. I'll show you some examples next; you should look for other examples at work and elsewhere.

Verification Instruments

One of the most authentic ways to assess learning (and transfer to the job) is to observe performance. To reduce subjectivity and improve the validity of the assessment, we often develop a checklist or rating scale for the skills we want to observe. Next are example portions of commonly used verification instruments.

A **checklist** lists observable behaviors or results.

Criteria	Fixes Required	Complete
List of job tasks that together comprise greater than or equal to 90% of work hours.		✓
List of job skills required to perform the listed job tasks.	"Technology skills" isn't specific enough. List the specific technology skills needed to	

Job Description Checklist

A **rating scale** offers a list of behaviors or results to be demonstrated with a description of the behavior or results. Descriptors tell learners and observers more precisely what performance looks like at each level.

Criteria	3 (Exceeds Standards)	2 (Meets Standards)	1 (Below Standards)	Score
Sections	Includes all appropriate sections: table of contents, executive summary, introduction, body, conclusions, references, appendices.	Few missing or mistitled sections that don't interfere with report organization	Many missing or mistitled sections, interferes with report organization	3 2 1

Report Format Rating Scale with Descriptors and Score

An **aggregate rating scale** gathers behaviors or results in groups, with a measurement scale to differentiate levels. Aggregate rating scales make sense in two situations. First, when a comprehensive judgment of total performance is more useful than judging individual criteria. Second, when it is difficult to evaluate performance on one measure independently of performance on a related measure (for example, writing clarity and organization).

3—Optimal	Diagnosed problem(s) within 5 minutes Clearly explained problem and required fix to client If parts available, fixed problem
2—Good	Diagnosed problem(s) in more than 5 minutes Didn't clearly explain problem or required fix to customer If parts available, fixed problem

Troubleshooting Aggregate Rating Scale

We develop checklists or rating scales using criteria that describe expected performance and results. For rating scales, labels (e.g., low, medium, high) show the degree to which the participant meets the criteria. A checklist or rating scale may include a mechanism for tallying a final "score."

Regarding levels, it often is better to start with fewer levels and then increase as needed. Differentiating between three or four levels is hard enough. As the number of levels increases, judgments become finer and finer, and the likelihood of error increases. Three levels may not capture all the variation in performance, but it may be adequate to capture the important variation in performance. Next is a rating scale template you can adapt for your own use.

Criteria	Levels			Score
	Developing 1	Proficient 2	Highly Skilled 3	
Behavior/ result	Description of observable behavior and results for this level of performance	Description of observable behavior and results for this level of performance	Description of observable behavior and results for this level of performance	
Behavior/ result	Description of observable behavior and results for this level of performance	Description of observable behavior and results for this level of performance	Description of observable behavior and results for this level of performance	
Behavior/ result	Description of observable behavior and results for this level of performance	Description of observable behavior and results for this level of performance	Description of observable behavior and results for this level of performance	
Behavior/ result	Description of observable behavior and results for this level of performance	Description of observable behavior and results for this level of performance	Description of observable behavior and results for this level of performance	
TOTAL				

Rating Scale Template

Assessment Simulations, Scenarios, Situations

It is often impractical or even undesirable to assess performance in the real world, so we may use high-fidelity simulations and scenarios to confirm or certify skills (Shrock & Coscarelli, 2007).

High-fidelity simulations reproduce real-world experiences in an immersive and interactive environment. The most familiar example of high-fidelity simulation is the flight simulator used to train pilots. Flight simulators reduce the cost and danger to train and assess pilots. Because of how realistic they are, pilots trained in flight simulators easily transition from practice flying to actual flying.

We use the term simulation to mean reproducing a real-life situation in a controlled "real world" environment. We typically use simulations to train people and assess whether they can act as needed in difficult and complex situations. They're used especially when adequate real-world practice and assessment isn't possible, isn't readily available, or is dangerous or cost prohibitive.

We use the term scenario to mean a realistic situation that prompts participants to make decisions using provided details. Scenarios involve less fidelity (realism) than simulations but are quite valuable for teaching and confirming skills (Shrock & Coscarelli, 2007).

We may present a scenario visually and with branching—different routes through the scenario based on participant actions. An example screen is below.

Visual branching scenario built in Articulate Rise, © Articulate Global, Inc., all rights reserved.

Scenarios can be less complex, with a textual description of the events and context as shown next.

Marta meets today with Juan about the centrifuge he wants to purchase. As his Q3 sales representative, Marta has met with him several times, including bringing the equipment to his lab for testing. She hoped to complete the sale today, but Juan seems unsure. When Marta asks him when he wants to take delivery, he answers, "It sure would help us out, but I'll never get it past the boss." Which of the following is the best response?
  a) Is cost your primary issue?
  b) Tell me more about that.

We can use simulations and scenarios for practice and assessment. When the assessment scenario is a multiple-choice question, I call them "situation questions." When you see situation questions in this book, I am talking about simpler scenarios using text descriptions and sometimes media such as images or documents.

"Test" Assessments

Test assessments use written or computerized test forms where learners select or enter answers to questions or prompts. There are two types: constructed-response and selected-response. Research shows that both types of tests, if well-constructed, can assess a wide variety of thought processes (Haladyna, 2013).

Constructed-response questions involve writing (constructing) an answer and are commonly short-answer and essay questions. Because responding to essays takes a lot of time, we cannot ask as many questions. As a result, they often can't assess a wide range of knowledge.

Selected-response questions can measure a wide variety of thought processes and learning objectives—such as recall of facts, understanding, and use. The most used selected response type is multiple-choice, and this is the type of question discussed in detail in this book.

Exercise Answers

Exercise 1-1. Does each learning objective make it obvious how to assess? What is the obvious way to assess the learning objective?

Learning objective	Is it obvious how to assess this objective?	What is the obvious way to assess this objective?
Understand the best navigation scheme for a website.	Yes **No**	Unclear. What exactly is the participant supposed to show that she can do?
Using the navigation evaluation checklist, find three websites that show appropriate navigation design.	**Yes** No	Find three websites that show appropriate navigation design, according to the checklist.
If a situation allows for time off, analyze whether it qualifies for paid or unpaid time off.	**Yes** No	Analyze whether permitted leave is paid or unpaid.

Exercise 1-2. Which of the following proposed changes to an assessment will improve validity? Which will improve reliability?

Proposed change	Improve validity?	Improve reliability?
Write clearly written questions.		✓
Make sure the items measure attainment of the objectives.	✓	
Increase the number of items for the most important objectives.	✓	
Improve wording clarity so items are easier to understand.		✓

Chapter Insights

Well-written multiple-choice questions allow us to:
- Efficiently measure a wide range of knowledge and skills.
- Easily and objectively score assessments.
- Assess concepts and principles, judgments, inferences, interpretation, application, and more.
- Reduce costs and time for assessment.
- Assess a representative sample of knowledge and skills.

Valid Assessments
- A valid assessment measures what it claims to measure.
- Reliability means the assessment works consistently.
- We are interested primarily in validity; we consider reliability because if the assessment isn't reliable, it isn't valid.

Criterion-Referenced Assessments
- Criterion-referenced assessments assess participants against specific criteria—the learning objectives.
- Well-written assessments are a proxy for directly observing people doing the job over time. When we write good assessments, they are suitable proxies for direct observation.

Performance vs. Test Assessments
- There are two primary formats for criterion-referenced assessments: performance assessments and test assessments. Assessments with multiple-choice questions are test assessments. They can assess a wide range of thought processes.
- Well-designed assessments come from well-designed test items (questions). Items that assess important knowledge and skills from the learning objectives make tests more valid.

Chapter References

Anderson, S. A. (1994). Synthesis of research on mastery learning. ERIC Information Analyses.

Black, P. J. & Wiliam, W. D. (2009). Developing the theory of formative assessment. Educational Assessment Evaluation and Accountability, 21(1), 5-31.

Brown, G. (2001). Assessment: A guide for lecturers. LTSN Generic Centre.

Brown, G., Bull, J. and Pendlebury, M. (1997). Assessing student learning in higher education. London: Routledge.

Coscarelli, W., Robins, D. G., Shrock, S., & Herbst, P. (1998). The certification suite: A classification system for certification tests. Performance Improvement 37(7), 13–18.

Drake Prometric. (1995). Certification for computing professionals. New York: McGraw Hill. Educational Testing Service. (2003). ETS fairness review guidelines. Princeton, NJ: Author.

Geertshuis, S., Holmes, M., Geertshuis, H., Clancy, D. and Bristol, A. (2002), Evaluation of workplace learning. Journal of Workplace Learning, 14(1), 11-18.

Gronlund, N. E. (1998). Assessment of student achievement, (6th ed). Boston, MA: Allyn and Bacon.

Guskey, T. & Pigott, T. (1988). Research on group-based mastery learning programs: A meta-analysis. Journal of Educational Research, 81(4), 197-216.

Haladyna, T. M. (2004). Developing and validating multiple-choice test items. Mahwah, NJ: Lawrence Erlbaum Associates, Inc.

Haladyna, T. M. & Rodriguez, M. (2013). Developing and Validating Test Items. New York: Routledge.

Hale, J. (2012). Performance-based certification: How to design a valid, defensible, cost-effective program (2nd ed.). San Francisco: Jossey-Bass/Pfeiffer.

Heinrich, R., Molenda, M., Russell, J. D., & Smaldino, S. E. (1996). Instructional media and technologies for learning. Englewood Cliffs, NJ: Merrill.

Impara, J. C.; Plake, B. S. (2000). A comparison of cut scores using multiple standard setting methods. Paper presented at the 81st Annual Meeting of the American Educational Research Association, New Orleans, LA.

Katzell, R. A. (1948). Testing a training program in human relations. Personnel Psychology, 1, 319-329.

Katzell, R. A. (1952). Can we evaluate training? A summary of a one-day conference for training managers. A publication of the Industrial Management Institute, University of Wisconsin, April 1952.

Kirkpatrick, D. L. (1959). Techniques for evaluating training programs. Journal of the American Society of Training Directors, 13(11), 3-9.

Kirkpatrick, D. L. (1959). Techniques for evaluating training programs: Part 2—Learning. Journal of the American Society of Training Directors, 13(12), 21-26.

Kirkpatrick, D. L. (1960). Techniques for evaluating training programs: Part 3—Behavior. Journal of the American Society of Training Directors, 14(1), 13-18.

Kirkpatrick, D. L. (1960b). Techniques for evaluating training programs: Part 4—Results. Journal of the American Society of Training Directors, 14(2), 28-32.

Koedinger, K. R., Corbett A. T., & Perfetti, C. (2012). The Knowledge-learning-instruction framework: Bridging the science-practice chasm to enhance robust student learning. Cognitive Science, 36(5).

Kulik, C., Kulik, J., & Bangert-Drowns, R. (1990). Effectiveness of mastery learning programs: A meta-analysis. Review of Educational Research, 60(2), 265-299.

Little, J., & Ligon Bjork, E. (2012). The persisting benefits of using multiple-choice tests as learning events. Proceedings of the Annual Meeting of the Cognitive Science Society, 34.

Marzano, R. J., Brandt, R. S., Hughes, C. S., Jones, B. F., Presseisen, B. Z., Rankin, S. C., & Suhor, C. (1988). Dimensions of thinking: A framework for curriculum and instruction. Alexandria, VA: Association for Supervision and Curriculum Development.

Marzano, R. J., Pickering, D. & McTighe, J. (1993). Assessing student outcomes. Alexandria, VA: Association for Supervision and Curriculum Development.

Mehrens, W. A., & Lehmann, I. J. (1973). Measurement and Evaluation in Education and Psychology. New York: Holt, Rinehart and Winston, 333-334.

Phillips, J. J. & Stone, R. D. (2002) How to measure training results: A practical guide to tracking the six key indicators. New York: McGraw-Hill.

Pittaway, L., Hannon, P., Gibb, A., & Thompson, J. (2009). Assessment practice in enterprise education. International Journal of Entrepreneurial Behavior & Research, 15(1), 71-93.

Renkl, A., Mandl, H. & Gruber, H. (1996). Inert knowledge: Analyses and remedies. Educational Psychologist, 31(2), 115-121.

Roediger, H. L., III, & Butler, A. C. (2011). The critical role of retrieval practice in long-term retention. Trends in Cognitive Sciences, 15, 20-27.

Shrock, S. A. & Coscarelli, W. C. (1998). Make the test match the job. Quality.

Shrock, S. A., & Coscarelli, W. C. (2007). Criterion-referenced test development: Technical and legal guidelines for corporate training and certification (3rd ed.). Silver Spring: Pfeiffer.

Thalheimer, W. (2018). The learning-transfer evaluation model: Sending messages to enable learning effectiveness.

Waugh, C. K. & Gronlund, N. E. (2013). Assessment of student achievement (10th ed.). Upper Saddle River, NJ: Pearson.

Chapter 2:
The Right Learning Objectives

Many people design and deliver instruction as a series of topics. They decide what they are going to teach, then decide how to teach those topics, then teach them. This approach has flaws, including delivering instruction that is less relevant or valuable. I'll describe what we need to do instead.

Outcomes Are Objectives

To design instruction with a list of topics is common, and often far less effective. To be effective, we should start with the outcomes needed from instruction (Gosling & Moon, 2001). When we use a topic approach, we tend to design content (information) rather than instruction designed to produce specific skills. We need to design for needed learning outcomes or what participants are expected to know, understand, and be able to do (Kennedy, Hyland, & Ryan, 2007). This is where learning objectives come in. They must describe exactly that.

Learning objectives are navigation tools, much like GPS. With GPS, we enter a destination, then GPS guides us there. Learning objectives guide us to activities and assessments to achieve the needed outcomes (Mahajan & Singh, 2017).

Well-written learning objectives have many benefits, including helping participants and other stakeholders analyze:

- Whether given instruction is relevant to their needs,
- What participants will be able to do, and
- The effort needed to achieve the specified outcomes (Kennedy, Hyland, & Ryan, 2007).

And well-written learning objectives help those who design and facilitate instruction to:

- Design instruction specifically to produce needed outcomes,
- Select needed content and activities to produce needed outcomes,
- Analyze what needs to be assessed,
- Design assessments specifically to measure needed outcomes, and
- Analyze whether instruction produces the needed outcomes.

Taylor's (2005) meta-analysis found that presenting learning outcomes as "rule codes" had a positive effect on knowledge used when performing a task. Rule codes are phrases that specifically describe what to do and why. For example, a rule code for adding new patients to the system might be, "Assure that patients are not already in the system to avoid duplicate entries." Rules codes are more impactful than less-specific statements such as, "Don't create duplicates."

We assume that "all objectives are at the use level (i.e., "performance" objectives) and that learners will practice or be assessed on the particular performance" (Sugrue, 2002). Sugrue explains that terminal and enabling objectives should always be written as performance objectives.

Terminal objectives describe what participants should be able to do as a result of instruction. Enabling objectives describe the sub-tasks for the task described in the terminal objective. For example, let's consider this terminal objective:

Accurately identify the meaning of medical terms used to describe a medical diagnosis.

Medical terminology is made up of roots, prefixes, and suffixes, so identifying their meaning depends on identifying the meaning of roots, prefixes, and suffixes and then putting them together. As a result, three enabling objectives for this terminal objective are:

Accurately identify the meaning of medical terminology roots used to describe a medical diagnosis.

Accurately identify the meaning of medical terminology prefixes used to describe a medical diagnosis.

Accurately identify the meaning of medical terminology suffixes used to describe a medical diagnosis.

The terminology "terminal objectives" and "enabling objectives" may be unfamiliar to you. Take the four learning objectives I just described. They tell us that participants need to be able to accurately identify the meanings of word parts (enabling objectives) and words made of those parts (terminal objective).

In some places in this book, I use "LO" to stand in for "learning objective."

Well-Written Learning Objectives

Learning objectives describe the specific real-life or job behaviors or actions needed from instruction and tell us how to measure them. For example, here's a well-written learning objective.

> **Content writers will write appropriate alternative text, which includes all needed elements, for each digital image.**

This learning objective is well written because it:
- Specifically describes what people must be able to do: Write alt text for a given digital image, AND
- Describes how to measure performance: Alt text is appropriate and includes all needed elements.

This learning objective points out what should be measured. Here are the two obvious things to measure:
- Do participants know the elements they need to include in alt text?
- Can participants write appropriate alt text for a given image that includes the needed elements?

> Before you develop well-written assessments, you must have well-written learning objectives. Otherwise, it's hard to know what to assess.

Sometimes someone gives you learning objectives that are poorly written (not real-life or job tasks, specific, or measurable). Poorly-written learning objectives provide little help in analyzing what assessments are needed and/or how to measure them.

If someone gives you poorly-written learning objectives, how can you write quality assessments to measure them? My advice? Rewrite them.

I totally get that you cannot simply change someone's learning objectives. But you do need to understand what their learning objectives should be to know what assessments are needed. For example, here is a learning objective a human resources manager gave me: "Understand how to manage staff tardiness."

Because this learning objective is not specific or measurable, here's the conversation we had that helped me rewrite it. At the end, you'll see the revised learning objective I used to write good multiple-choice questions.

Me: What do you want people to be able to do when you say in your learning objective that people should understand how to manage staff tardiness?

HR Manager: I want them to know what to do.

Who needs to know what to do?

Supervisors.

You want supervisors to know what to do in which circumstances?

I want them to know what to do when a staff member is tardy.

You want supervisors to know what to do when a staff member comes to work after the time they were scheduled to arrive?

Yes. That's right

What do supervisors need to do when a staff member comes to work after the time they were scheduled to arrive?

They need to do what the tardiness policy says.

Which is what?

It depends on how many times they've been late and whether the lateness is because of one of the two exceptions.

So, they need to apply the tardiness policy based on how many times a staff member has been late and follow the two exceptions. Correct?

Yes. Why all the questions?

Knowing the specifics of what people must be able to do will help me write relevant multiple-choice questions for your course.

Oh. Great.

The resulting LO: Supervisors will use the tardiness policy to correctly apply the consequences for staff tardiness.

You may not be able to literally rewrite someone else's learning objectives but knowing what they should be will help you write good multiple-choice questions.

Rothwell & Kazanas (2008) describe how task analysis (the analysis of work tasks and how they are performed) informs the writing of learning objectives, as shown below.

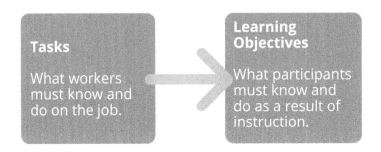

To write LOs, use what people know and do in real life and on the job to inform what needs to be assessed.

MORE...

I recommend this book to help you better understand task analysis.

Wallace, G. (2021). The 3 Ds of ThoughtFlow Analysis: Task Analysis for Instructional Development.

To maintain the URLs more easily for online resources, they are available here: https://www.pattishank.com/mcqresources

ABCD Learning Objectives

The ABCD method of writing learning objectives helps us understand who is performing, what they are doing, the context in which they are doing it, and the outcomes needed. (Heinrich et al., 1996). The ABCD method asks us to analyze:

Audience
Describe the target audience, so you can pinpoint their specific tasks and outcomes.

Behavior
Describe the behavior or action using an action verb matching real-life or job tasks.

Context
Describe the circumstances under which the target audience performs. May include when and where the task is performed and with what tools and resources.

Degree
Describe how well the task must be done or what outcomes must be achieved. May include speed, accuracy, timeliness, completeness, quantity, quality, etc.

Next are three examples of analyzing the ABCDs for learning objectives.

Example 1

Audience	Behavior/Action	Context	Degree/Outcome
bystander	perform cardiac defibrillation	on an unresponsive cardiac-arrest victim	correctly
		following the commands of an AED machine	

LO: On an unresponsive cardiac-arrest victim, the bystander will correctly use an AED machine to perform defibrillation following the AED commands.

Example 2

Audience	Behavior/Action	Context	Degree/Outcome
staff who travel	complete an expense report	using the corporate travel application	within 15 days of returning to home base
			without errors

LO: Within 15 days of returning to home base, staff who travel will complete their expense reports in the corporate travel application without errors.

Example 3

Audience	Behavior/Action	Context	Degree/Outcome
students	solve geometry problems	using the Pythagorean Theorem	8 out of 10 correct answers

LO: Students will correctly solve at least 8 out of 10 geometry problems using the Pythagorean Theorem.

TRY THIS!

Exercise 2-1. For the situation below, analyze the ABCDs.

I completed the first item to show you how to do the exercise.

Exercise answers are at the end of this chapter. You will learn more if you do the exercise *before* you review the answers.

Situation: Front-lobby staff should make a digital copy of acceptable visitor identification when visitors arrive. The staff should date the digital copies and appropriately file them in the required secure digital location.

Audience: Front-lobby staff

Behavior:

Context:

Degree:

Action Verbs in Learning Objectives

Selecting an action verb (the B in ABCD) is an important part of writing good learning objectives. Many times, however, we have a hard time selecting the right one and pick one that isn't accurate or precise. To me, it's essential to choose an accurate and precise action verb—because it describes what we are going to assess. We've made this task more difficult than it needs to be.

Think about the following words: "appreciate" and "understand." These don't describe real-life or job tasks and they aren't measurable. Simply put, we shouldn't use them. These, and similar, words—e.g., define, describe, explain, and list—often don't describe real-life or job tasks, either. Unless this is what people need to be able to do, we shouldn't use them.

The medical terminology terminal and enabling objectives I wrote earlier use the action verb, "identify." I selected "identify" rather than "list" or "describe" because it is what people actually must do.

There are some real-life or job tasks that involve defining, describing, explaining, or listing. When you check into a hotel, for example, the front desk agent explains how to get to the elevator, find the pool, or locate the concierge. For enabling objectives, it is common to use the action verb "define" because a definition is often a sub-task of learning a new task.

Too often, though, we use "list" (or define, describe, or explain) when people are really doing something else. For example, we may write "List how to" when, in real life or on the job, they are doing the thing they are asked to list in the assessment. Instead, use an action verb that describes what the person actually does.

> In many cases, the choice of an action verb should be quite simple. Describe what the person is doing in real life when they perform the task.

TRY THIS!

Exercise 2-2. In the left column of this exercise, I describe what four people do in real life or on the job. Select the most accurate and precise action verb to describe what they do. This should be easy.

Then select an action verb for the two harder situations. This will be less easy.

I completed the first item to show you how to do the exercise.

Exercise answers are at the end of this chapter. You will learn more if you do the exercise *before* you review the answers.

What they are doing:	What is the action verb?
Maria writes a report.	Write
Dion edits a graphic.	
Rakesh calculates the mean.	
Raya negotiates a sale.	

Now try an example where selecting a precise action verb is a bit harder.

What they are doing:	What is the action verb?
Aran looks at the HTML code for existing website images to see if they have appropriate alt tags or text.	
Thérèse works with a potential customer to figure out their needs and buying constraints.	

REAL-LIFE AND JOB-TASK ACTION VERBS

The following list of action verbs, from job descriptions, describe real-life tasks. Don't use "understand" or "appreciate." Avoid "define," "describe," "explain," and "list," unless that's what the person is doing in real life or on the job and that's what you need to assess. They are divided into two levels of thinking: understand and use. I discuss these levels in more detail in Chapter 4.

Understand	Use		
categorize	acquire	design	modify
choose	administer	develop	negotiate
identify	advise	direct	notify
paraphrase	analyze	distribute	order
summarize	approve	document	organize
	arrange	draft	plan
	assemble	edit	predict
	assess	establish	prepare
	assist	estimate	present
	authorize	evaluate	prevent
	build	facilitate	process
	calculate	finalize	produce
	certify	find	provide
	check	flag	purchase
	clarify	follow up	recommend
	code	guide	record
	collaborate	help	recruit
	collect	hire	resolve
	communicate	implement	respond
	complete	inform	review
	conduct	inspect	revise
	confirm	install	schedule
	contribute	interpret	solve
	counsel	investigate	submit
	create	issue	supply
	compare	listen	update
	coordinate	maintain	verify
	decide	manage	write
	deliver	measure	use

From Learning Objectives to Questions

Once we have specific and measurable ABCD learning objectives, we can analyze them to find important and relevant multiple-choice questions. For example, consider the following learning objective:

Workers will wear appropriate personal protective equipment (PPE) for outdoor construction tasks.

What does the learning objective suggest are important knowledge and skill questions that participants should be able to answer? Here are a few especially important questions—you can probably think of others.

- What injuries are most likely when [construction situation]?
- What PPE is needed for [this task]?
- What if the [needed PPE] isn't available?

The table below shows these three questions and corresponding relevant multiple-choice stems to assess them. You can see how these questions help us write relevant multiple-choice questions.

Question	Relevant multiple-choice question stems
What injuries are most likely when [construction situation]?	[Situation] Which injury is most likely? Example: You're working with foam insulation. Which injury do you need to protect yourself from?
What PPE do you need for [this task]?	[Situation] What PPE should you use to prevent [injury type]? Example: You're working around the following machinery: jackhammers, sledgehammers, and electric saws. Which PPE will help you prevent hearing loss?
What if the [needed PPE] isn't available?	[Situation] What should you do if [needed PPE] isn't available? Example: Electricians are working with high voltage nearby. You don't have a Class E hardhat. What is the best thing to do to protect yourself in this situation?

When I teach others to list questions that participants should be able to answer, they often come up with who, what, when, where, how, and why questions. They often forget "what if" questions.

"What ifs" ask about common issues and dilemmas when performing the learning objective task. Make sure to consider "what ifs." Making the right decision when dealing with problems is often quite important!

For example, here are some "what if" questions we may need to ask about filing an expense report after returning from work travel.

- What if I don't submit the report on time?
- What if I get [error] when filing my report?
- What if I don't have all my receipts when filing my report?

TRY THIS!

Exercise 2-3. Below is a learning objective and two questions to assess the learning objective. For each question, write a multiple-choice stem to assess whether participants have the needed knowledge and skills to answer this question.

I completed the first item to show you how to do the exercise.

Exercise answers are at the end of this chapter. You will learn more if you do the exercise *before* you review the answers.

LO: Employees will notify appropriate staff when they see applicable safety hazards in the building.

Question	Multiple-choice question stem
Who are the appropriate staff to notify?	Who should Laura notify about a potential electrical safety hazard?
Which safety hazards require notifying appropriate staff?	

Exercise Answers

Exercise 2-1. For the situation below, use the ABCD method to write the ABCDs.

Situation: Front desk staff should make a digital copy of acceptable visitor identification when visitors arrive. The staff should date the digital copies and appropriately file them in the required secure digital location.

Audience: Front desk staff
Behavior: Make a digital copy of visitor identification
Context: When visitors visit
Degree: Acceptable identification, digital copy, dated, filed in secure digital location

Exercise 2-2. In the left column of this exercise, I describe what four people do in real life or on the job. Select the most accurate and precise action verb to describe what they do. This should be easy. Then select an action verb for the two harder situations. This will be less easy.

What they do:	What is the action verb?
Maria writes a report.	Write
Dion edits a graphic.	Edit
Rakesh calculates the mean.	Calculate
Raya negotiates a sale.	Negotiate

What they do:	What is the action verb?
Aran looks at the HTML code for existing website images to see if they have appropriate alt tags or text.	Check? Review?
Thérèse works with a potential customer to figure out their needs and buying constraints.	Ask? Listen? Analyze?

Exercise 2-3. Below is a learning objective and two questions to assess the learning objective. For each question, write a multiple-choice stem to assess whether participants have the needed knowledge and skills to answer this question.

LO: Employees will notify appropriate staff when they see applicable safety hazards in the building.

Question	Multiple-choice question stem
Who are the appropriate staff to notify?	Who should Laura notify about a potential electrical safety hazard?
Which safety hazards require notifying appropriate staff?	Laura is using the copier and notices that the copier electrical cord is plugged into an extension cord which is plugged into a wall outlet. Is this a safety hazard that requires notification?

Chapter Insights

Objectives
- Learning outcomes are statements of what we expect participants to know, understand, and be able to do. This is what learning objectives describe.
- Learning objectives convey many benefits. Some of the most important are telling stakeholders the outcomes expected from instruction, selecting content and activities to meet those outcomes, informing formative and summative assessments, and determining if instruction is producing the needed results.

Well-Written Learning Objectives
- Well-written learning objectives describe valuable real-life or job behaviors and are specific and measurable.
- To write good learning objectives, you need to know what people do in real life or on the job.

ABCD Learning Objectives
- ABCD learning objectives are performance based, task focused, and can inform relevant multiple-choice objectives.
- An ABCD learning objective describes who does the task, what they specifically need to do, the circumstances under which the task must be done, when to do the task, what information or tools are used to do the task, and how well the task must be done or what outcome must be achieved.
- For the B in ABCD learning objectives, we need to use a verb that describes what the person does when performing the learning objective task.

From Learning Objectives to Questions
- Participants who have achieved the learning objectives should be able to answer specific questions. Analyze the LO to identify those questions. Use these questions to write relevant multiple-choice questions.

Chapter References

Anderson, L. W. & Krathwohl, D. R. (Eds.). (2001). A taxonomy for learning, teaching, and assessing: A revision of bloom's taxonomy of educational objectives. New York: Longman.

Decker, P. J. (1980). Effects of symbolic coding and rehearsal in behavior modeling training. Journal of Applied Psychology, 65, 627–634.

Decker, P. J. & Nathan, B. R. (1985). Behavior modeling training: Principles and applications. New York: Praeger.

Glaser R. & Nitko, A. J. (1971). Measurement in learning and instruction. In R. L. Thorndike (Ed.) Educational measurement (2nd ed). Washington, DC: American Council on Education.

Gosling, D. & Moon, J. (2001) How to Use Learning Outcomes and Assessment Criteria. London: SEEC Office.

Heinrich, R., Molenda, M., Russell, J. D., Smaldino, S. E. (1996). Instructional media and technologies for learning. Englewood Cliffs, NJ: Merrill.

Hoffman, C. K. & Medsker, K. L. (1983). Instructional analysis: The missing link between task analysis and objectives. Journal of Instructional Development, 6(17).

Hopkins, K. D. (1998). Educational and psychological measurement and evaluation. Needham Heights, MA: Allyn & Bacon.

Jonassen, D. H. & Hannum, W. H. (1986). Analysis of task analysis procedures. Journal of Instructional Development, 9(2), 2-12.

Kennedy, D., Hyland, A., & Ryan, N. (2007). Writing and using learning outcomes: a practical guide.

Koedinger, K. R., Corbett A. T., & Perfetti, C. (2012). The knowledge-learning-instruction framework: Bridging the science-practice chasm to enhance robust student learning. Cognitive Science, 36(5).

Krathwohl, D. R. (2002). A revision of Bloom's taxonomy: An overview. Theory into Practice, 41(4), 212-218.

Mahajan, M. & Singh, M. K. S. (2017). Importance and benefits of learning outcomes. IOSR Journal of Humanities and Social Science, 22(3), 65-67.

Mager, R. F. (1975). Preparing instructional objectives. (2nd ed.). Belmont, CA: Fearon.

Marzano, R. J. (2001). Designing a new taxonomy of educational objectives. Experts in Assessment. Thousand Oaks, CA: Corwin Press, Inc.

Renkl, A., Mandl, H., & Gruber, H. (1996). Inert knowledge: Analyses and remedies. Educational Psychologist, 31(2), 115-121.

Rothwell, W. J. & Kazanas, H. C. (2008). Mastering the Instructional Design Process. San Francisco: Pfeiffer.

Simon, B. & Taylor, J. (2009). What is the value of course-specific learning goals? Journal of College Science Teaching, 39(2), 52.

Sugrue, B. (2002). Problems with Bloom's taxonomy.

Sugrue, B. (2013). A learning science alternative to Bloom's taxonomy. Learning Solutions Magazine.

Taylor, P. J., Russ-Eft, D. F., & Chan, D. W. L. (2005). A meta-analytic review of behavior modeling training. Journal of Applied Psychology, 90(4), 692–709.

Chapter 3:
Write Multiple-Choice Questions

n this chapter, we'll discuss the parts of a multiple-choice question and how to write them correctly.

Parts of a Multiple-Choice Question

Multiple-choice questions include a **stem** and **answer choices**. The stem asks the question, and answer choices include the correct answer (key) and incorrect but plausible answers (distractors). The most common multiple-choice question type includes a stem, one key, and two or more distractors. Here is the typical format for a multiple-choice question and an example of a multiple-choice question in this typical format.

Stem
    a)   Answer choice
    b)   Answer choice
    c)   Answer choice

Which of the following image formats is best to use for digital images that require frequent resizing?
    a)   JPG - Joint Photographic Experts Group
    b)   EPS - Encapsulated Postscript *
    c)   PNG - Portable Network Graphics

> Multiple-choice question writers often use an asterisk (*) to indicate the correct answer for each question.

Other multiple-choice question formats are discussed in Chapter 5. Multiple-choice questions may include media, such as images, audio, or video, which are used to offer information needed to select the correct answer(s). Media use is discussed in Chapter 3.

Stem

Good stems ask about relevant and important knowledge or skills in the learning objective. Consider what important knowledge and skill is most relevant to assess for the following learning objective.

Within 15 days of returning to home base, staff who travel will complete their expense reports in the corporate travel application without errors.

In Chapter 2, I discussed analyzing the most important questions a participant should be able to answer for each learning objective. Here are important questions I think participants should be able to answer for this learning objective.

- When must I complete an expense report?
- What if I don't complete my expense report within the specified time?
- How do I complete an expense report?
- How can I tell if the expense report has any errors?
- What if I receive an error code while completing the report?

To review the process for using these questions to create relevant multiple-choice question stems, I'll show how I would use some of these questions to write stems. For example, I could use this question to assess whether test takers understand when they must complete an expense report.

If you return from a trip on the 10th of the month, which of these dates is the last date you can file your expense report?

I could use this question to assess whether test takers know what will happen if the expense report isn't completed within the specified time.

Which of the following is a consequence of submitting your expense report after the allotted time period?

I could use variations of the following stem to assess whether participants can tell if the expense report has any errors.

[expense report image] **What error is shown on this expense report screen?**

Good Stems

Below are two stems. The top stem is incomplete and doesn't communicate what we are assessing. The bottom stem is complete and does communicate what we are assessing. Stems *must* clearly communicate what we are assessing.

Workplace fires: (Doesn't communicate what is being tested.)

If you encounter a workplace fire, what is the first thing you should do? (Communicates what is being tested.)

The two best formats for a stem are a **question** and an **incomplete sentence**. The following is the same stem written as a question and as an incomplete sentence.

There is a small fire in the wastebasket next to a desk. When should you clear the building? (Question)

There is a small fire in the wastebasket next to a desk. You should clear the building when: (Incomplete sentence)

A good stem has the following characteristics.

Concise	Phrase the stem in as few words as possible using easy-to-understand words and sentences.
Positively stated	Avoid words such as NOT, ISN'T, and DON'T because they make the stem harder to understand and answer. State the stem positively instead.
Includes only relevant details	Include enough details in the stem to understand what is being tested. Leave out irrelevant information. If the learning objective requires finding irrelevant information, use a situation-based question.

Uses "should" instead of "could"	When the stem uses "could," participants are more likely to select partly correct answer choices. Use of "should" helps people select the correct or best answer and not a partially or sometimes correct answer.
Offers no clues	We should not offer any clues or hints as to the correct answer in the stem.
Doesn't retell	The stem should not repeat instructional content. It should prompt people to use previous content.

TRY THIS!

Exercise 3-1. For the two learning objectives shown (left column), write a stem that assesses important knowledge and skills.

I completed the first item to show you how to do the exercise.

Exercise answers are at the end of this chapter. You will learn more if you do the exercise *before* you review the answers.

Learning Objective	Stem
Students will calculate the mean score from a series of test scores.	Calculate the mean score from the following test scores.
Technicians will select the appropriate personal protective equipment for a given pesticide application situation.	

Answer Choices

Answer choices include the correct answer (the **key**) and the plausible but incorrect answers (the **distractors**). People who know the content being tested should be able to select the correct or best answer. And they should be able to tell that the distractors are either:

- Not best or completely correct,
- Only sometimes correct, or
- Incorrect.

Good distractors should be plausible to people who do not know the content being tested. Poorly-written distractors often help those who don't know the content to guess the correct answer as they can easily eliminate obviously incorrect answers. We want to avoid making it easier to guess correctly. Good answer choices have the following characteristics.

Clear and concise	Answer choices must be easy to understand. Complex and wordy language and sentences test ability to understand poor writing, which is usually not what we want to test.
Similar length and detail	All answer choices should be of similar length and contain the same level of detail. People know that an answer that is longer or has more detail is often the correct answer.
Follow from the stem	All answer choices should follow grammatically from the stem. For example, if an incomplete sentence stem ends in "an," we know the correct answer starts with a vowel.
Logical order	If the answer choices have a logical order (for example, date or quantity), answer choices should appear in that order.

Parallel construction	Answers should ideally start with the same part of speech ("consider," "analyze," "select" rather than "consider," "analyzing," "the").
Avoids absolutes	It is easier to dismiss answers that include "never," "none," "all," or "always," as absolutes tend not to be true. Avoid absolutes!

Distractors

Well-written multiple-choice questions allow us to distinguish between those with the needed knowledge and skill and those without it. For this to occur, distractors, or incorrect answer choices, must be attractive as potential correct answers for participants who don't have the needed knowledge and skill.

For distractors to work as intended, they must be plausible. Implausible distractors make it easier to guess the correct answer. In this example, try to guess which distractor is not plausible.

What will happen if you try to log into the application with an incorrect password three times within an hour? (Select the correct answer.)

a)	You will lose access to the account for 24 hours.	Correct answer
b)	You will lose access to the account for 72 hours.	Distractor
c)	Your account will disappear into a puff of smoke.	Distractor

The example has one distractor that is clearly not plausible, and you probably guessed that the implausible distractor is answer c. This implausible answer choice makes it easier to guess that answer a or b is the correct answer. In Chapter 7, I discuss in more detail why guessing is a problem.

> The #1 rule of writing good distractors is that the distractor must be plausible to those who don't know the content. Distractors also need to be incorrect or not best to those who do know the content.

Gierl (2017) suggests additional rules for writing good distractors:
- Avoid none-of-the-above and all-of-the-above as answer choices.
- Avoid offering clues as to the correct answer.
- Use the same grammatical structure for all answer choices.
- Phrase distractors positively.

Best Distractors

Researchers suggest creating distractors from common misconceptions and errors in thinking and from paraphrasing the correct answer incorrectly (Gierl et al., 2017; Shin et al., 2019; Haladyna, 2004). I'll discuss these two tactics for writing distractors next.

Misconceptions as Distractors

To create distractors from misconceptions and errors in thinking, we first must find common misconceptions and errors in thinking! If you are a content expert, you likely know them. For example, I know that a common misconception about multiple-choice questions is that they only measure recall. If I were writing this stem—"Are multiple-choice questions good for assessing decision making?"—one distractor I'd use is:

No, because multiple-choice questions primarily assess recall.

If you are not a content expert, though, you may not know common misconceptions. To find them, you can:
- Build a list of common incorrect participant responses from prior activities such as discussions and open-ended polls.
- Ask proficient performers and other competent content specialists what misconceptions, mistakes, and errors people with incomplete or inaccurate knowledge commonly make. To be specific, we may ask, "What are common mistakes or errors that less-expert people make when doing [task] or solving [problem]?"
- Ask workers about the misconceptions they had earlier on.

Next are two example questions that use common misconceptions as distractors.

Example 1

Medical errors are a leading cause of death. Research shows that the primary reason we are unable to prevent all medical errors is: (Select the best answer.)
   a) Failure to allocate adequate resources.
   b) The limitations of people and technologies. *
   c) Reluctance to change existing procedures.

Answers a and c are common misconceptions. They have merit, but they don't answer the question about the primary reason we are unable to prevent all medical errors. Only b answers the specific question.

Example 2

Which of the following theories correctly explains how airplanes can fly? (Select the correct answer.)
   a) Air flow on the top of the wing is faster than on the bottom.
   b) Air molecules hitting the bottom of the wing push the wing.
   c) Aerodynamic forces oppose the airplane's weight as it flies. *

The correct answer to this question is c. Answers a and b are common misconceptions.

One benefit of using common misconceptions and errors as distractors in multiple-choice questions is that assessment results help us understand participant misconceptions so we can fix them! This is especially valuable for formative assessment. We can also use these results to inform revisions to instruction after summative assessment.

Incorrect Paraphrasing as Distractors

Another approach to write good distractors is to make them similar to the correct answer *but incorrect*. A common way to implement this tactic is to start with the correct answer and vary it to be incorrect but plausible. We can implement this strategy easily by replacing parts of the correct answer.

Next are two examples. First is the correct answer, and then two ways you might incorrectly paraphrase the correct answer for plausible distractors.

Example 1

Correct	The court clerk will collect the licensing fee and issue the license the same day.
Incorrectly paraphrased	The judicial assistant will collect the licensing fee and issue the license the same day.
Incorrectly paraphrased	The court clerk will collect the licensing fee and mail the license within 5-7 days.

Example 2

Correct	You will lose access to the account for 24 hours.
Incorrectly paraphrased	You will lose access to the account for 72 hours.
Incorrectly paraphrased	You will lose access to information in Tiers 1-3.

Try This!

Exercise 3-2. For the stem and correct answer below, write an incorrectly paraphrased distractor.

I completed one distractor to help you see how to do the exercise.

Exercise answers are at the end of this chapter. You will learn more if you do the exercise *before* you review the answers.

Stem:
You are inputting a new vendor into the vendor database. You are in a hurry and don't add the vendor's address. Which of the following is an important consequence of not inputting the vendor address information at the time of vendor setup? (Select the best answer.)

Correct answer:
The vendor will not appear in regional sales reports.

My distractor:
The vendor will not receive notice of account setup.

Your distractor?

Here are two examples of multiple-choice questions which use misconceptions and incorrect paraphrasing for distractors.

Example 1

Stem:
Nia must wash her hands before she comes back after a break. The handwashing sink has run out of hot water. What should she do? (Select the correct answer.)

Correct answer	Use cold water to wash her hands.
Distractor: Misconception	Wait for hot water to wash her hands.
Distractor: Paraphrased incorrectly	Use the prep sink to wash her hands.

Example 2

Stem:
The toxicity of which one of these three routes of entry—inhalation, eyes, skin—determines the pesticide signal word? (Select the correct answer.)

Correct answer	The route of entry that has the highest toxicity
Distractor: Misconception	The "average" toxicity by the three routes of entry
Distractor: Paraphrased incorrectly	The route of entry most typical for the pesticide

The correct answer often offers hints about the plausible distractors to use. For example, if the correct answer is, "Moderately toxic," what are obvious choices for distractors? I might incorrectly paraphrase the correct answer and use "Nontoxic" and "Extremely toxic."

TRY THIS!

Exercise 3-3. For the three correct answers shown (left column), write a distractor that incorrectly paraphrases the correct answer.

I completed the first item to show you how to do the exercise.

Exercise answers are at the end of this chapter. You will learn a lot more if you do the exercise *before* you review the answers.

Correct answer	Distractors
A fire extinguisher rated for grease fires.	A fire extinguisher rated for paper fires.
Replace with a part with the exact same part number.	
30 days after enrolling	

None of the Above and All of the Above

Research shows that all-of-the-above (AOTA) and none-of-the-above (NOTA) perform poorly as answer choices and we should not use them.

NOTA is a bad answer choice because, when NOTA is the correct answer, the question provides us with little information about what the participant knows. Why would we do that? In addition, if participants can find one answer they know is correct, they can eliminate NOTA as the correct answer. Test-wise participants know that NOTA is usually a throwaway, which helps them eliminate the answer and more effectively guess.

AOTA is usually a bad answer choice because, if participants can find one answer they know is incorrect, they can eliminate AOTA as the correct answer (which means they eliminated two of the answer choices). Test-wise participants know that AOTA is often the correct answer, which helps them guess more successfully.

When tempted to use these answer choices, rethink the question. For example, if NOTA is correct, ask about what to do rather than what not to do. If AOTA is correct, use a multiple-correct question (see Chapter 5).

Same Length Answer Choices

People who take my classes often ask me how I make all answers the same length. The short answer is, "It takes lots of practice." The longer answer is, "There's a back-and-forth process I use to write concise distractors that are all of similar length."

The primary tactic is to add and subtract words from answer choices until they are the same length and concise. With lots of practice, this gets easier. Here's my typical process.

1. Write the stem and the correct answer choice. I intentionally try to make the correct answer concise, which makes the process easier.
2. Write the distractors.
3. Check the length of the distractors compared to the correct answer. If it differs, adjust answers to make them the same length.
4. When I can't make the correct answer and the distractors the same length, I add or subtract words from answer choices until they are the same length.
5. Sometimes I need to edit the stem to get concise, same-length answer choices.

To show you how I do this, I'll show the actual process I use for writing a question.

Stem
Mia's staff member, Brian, regularly leaves for lunch with an outside vendor, Olivia. Brian is Olivia's purchasing agent and makes purchasing decisions about products from Olivia's company. Mia is worried that their relationship may be influencing his decisions. What should she do first? (Select the best answer.)

Correct answer
Read the Employee Code of Conduct policy to figure out whether the vendor relationship is a problem that needs to be fixed.

Distractors
Here's my first attempt at writing distractors. I am using two common misunderstandings for the distractors.
- Say and do nothing because their relationship is not her business and meddling could cause harm.
- Discuss the issue with the human resources department.

I am pretty sure the answers are not the same length. Lining them up provides a fast visual.
- Read the Employee Code of Conduct policy to determine whether the vendor relationship is a problem that needs to be fixed. *
- Say and do nothing because their relationship is not her business and meddling could cause harm.
- Discuss the issue with the human resources department.

As expected, they are not all the same length. I also notice that the correct answer and the first distractor are quite long and need to be more concise. Here's the new shorter correct answer.

Read the Employee Code of Conduct to find out if the relationship is prohibited.

It took me three tries to get a, b, and c the same length.

Try 1

   a) Read the Employee Code of Conduct to find out if the relationship is prohibited. *
   b) Say and do nothing because their relationship is not her business.
   c) Ask her human resources partner to find out if this relationship is prohibited.

Answer a and c are now similar length, but likely longer than needed. New shorter correct answer:

Read the Employee Code of Conduct to clarify prohibited actions.

Try 2

   a) Read the Employee Code of Conduct to clarify prohibited actions. *
   b) Take no actions because their relationship is not her business.
   c) Ask her human resources partner to find out if this is a problem.

They are all closer in length, but answer c is unclear.

Try 3

   a) Read the Employee Code of Conduct to clarify prohibited actions. *
   b) Take no actions because their relationship is not her business.
   c) Ask her human resources partner if this relationship is prohibited.

Finally. They are all close to the same length—and clear.

In a few cases, making answers the same length makes no sense. If the answers are names of actual things, the length of each answer will depend on the length of the name. For example, here are four answers to a question about selecting interior settings for a self-published book. They need to be different lengths because they are the actual names of specific options.
   a) Paperback, black-and-white interior
   b) Paperback, color interior
   c) Hard cover, black-and-white interior
   d) Hard cover, color interior

Number of Answer Choices

Conventional wisdom says the more answer choices we offer for a multiple-choice question the better. A quick analysis of probabilities says that a multiple-choice question with five answer choices gives the test taker a 20% chance of randomly guessing the correct answer. A question with four answer choices gives the test taker a 25% chance of randomly guessing the correct answer.

Recent research shows that simple probabilities do not get at the actual differences between three- or four- or five-answer multiple-choice questions. Researchers now recommend three answer choices (one correct answer and two incorrect answers) in most cases (Haladyna, 2019; Rodriguez, 2005; Vyas, 2008).

Since writing good distractors is difficult, creating more distractors just to fill in answer slots often creates lower-quality questions with implausible distractors that are easy to pick out as incorrect.

> Research explains that distractor quality is much more critical to question quality than the number of distractors.

Writing plausible distractors is usually the most difficult part of writing multiple-choice questions. It takes question writers less time to write three well-written answer choices and it takes test takers less time to read and answer three well-written answer choices. As a result, writing three well-written answer choices means test writers can write more and better questions—and assessments can include more questions. Better distractors and more test questions can increase test validity. Score!

The bottom line is that offering three answer options offers many advantages and performs as well as (and sometimes better than) four- and five-answer options.

If this advice worries you, as it did me when I first researched it, read the meta-analysis below and you may you feel better about it, as I did. I now write three answers in most cases for my multiple-choice questions.

You can use more than three answer choices, of course, if all distractors are plausible. It's also okay to use a different number of answer choices for different questions.

MORE...

The following research discusses the evidence for using fewer answer choices.

Rodriguez, M. C. (2005). Three options are optimal for multiple-choice items: A meta-analysis of 80 years of research. Educational Measurement Issues and Practice, 24(2), 3 – 13.

To maintain the URLs more easily for online resources, they are available here: https://www.pattishank.com/mcqresources

How Many Multiple-Choice Questions?

Everything else being equal—which is rarely the case—we can improve the validity of a test by adding questions that more completely assess needed knowledge and skills. There are nuances, of course. For example, adding trivial questions does not improve assessments, as adding implausible distractors does not improve questions.

Shrock & Coscarelli (2007) say we achieve "the balance between effectiveness and efficiency in item numbers at four to six items per objective, but we know more items are required for some critical objectives."

They offer a table as a rough estimate of how many items to include per objective, while reminding us, "...the actual reliability and validity of the test can only be determined after some test results have been collected."

If the objectives are			Estimated number of items per objective
Critical	From a large domain	Unrelated	10-20
		Related	10
	From a small domain	Unrelated	5-10
		Related	5
Not critical	From a large domain	Unrelated	6
		Related	4
	From a small domain	Unrelated	2
		Related	1

From Shrock & Coscarelli (2007). *Criterion-Referenced Test Development*, third edition, page 171, used with Bill Coscarelli's permission

An article written by Questionmark, a well-known enterprise assessment platform, tells us we need to balance the number of items needed with time constraints for taking the assessment. For example, the article offers the following table that shows the average amount of time needed for different question formats.

Question Format	Amount of Time
Multiple-choice	1 to 1½ minutes
Matching	30 seconds per response
Short answer	2 minutes
Added image	Add 30 seconds

From https://www.questionmark.com/test-design-and-delivery-part-3-final-planning-considerations, used with permission.

As you can see, even if we don't place time constraints on an assessment, we need to consider the time an assessment is likely to take.

Media Use

Shrock & Coscarelli (1998) tell us to "[W]rite questions that imitate the way the employee receives data and solves problems in real life." This suggests we should show what the person sees and hears when relevant to the task.

Next are three examples of media use in questions. In each example, media allows participants to see or hear as they see or hear in real life.

Example 1

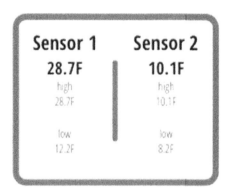

When you opened the restaurant this morning, the temperature gauge on the backup refrigerator read as shown. What should you do first? (Select the best answer.)

    a.   Confirm the internal temperature with the ThermoXV. *
    b.   Move perishables to another, working refrigerator.
    c.   Request an urgent service call to fix the problem.

Example 2

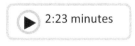
Play the call to hear the customer's problem. What emotion do you hear? (Select the correct answer.)

    a.   Sadness
    b.   Frustration *
    c.   Anger

Example 3

Play the video showing Nia washing her hands at the start of her shift. What does Nia do that violates the hand washing guidelines? (Select the correct answer.)

    a.   She doesn't scrub for 20 seconds.
    b.   She doesn't rinse adequately. *
    c.   She doesn't dry her hands.

Avoid using non-relevant (decorative) images, audio, and video, of course, as it uses mental effort needed to answer the question. We should use media because it is valuable for the assessment and make it accessible so it can be used by a wide diversity of users.

Understandability

The mental process needed to answer questions is complex. The first task is to interpret the question to understand what it means and what is being asked (Sudman, Bradburn, & Schwarz, 1996). When assessments are hard to understand, they are less valid and less fair. We cannot assess achievement of the learning objectives if participants cannot understand the questions or the instructions.

Making assessments understandable is important for everyone. Some participants will have a much harder time understanding the assessment if test questions and instructions aren't clear. People taking tests in a language other than their primary language will have problems with language complexity. Making tests more understandable also helps people taking tests in their primary language, because test takers have different reading comprehension levels (Haladyna & Rodriguez, 2013).

Language complexity negatively affects assessment outcomes and leaves us with a less-valid picture of what test takers know and can do (Abedi, 2006). In my experience with field testing items before using them, I regularly find questions that are hard to understand. Here are important ways to improve understandability.

Use high-frequency words.

Use common words that are more widely understood. Use simple words rather than complex words with the same meaning. An example of simpler wording is "use" instead of "utilize." Shorter, simpler, more familiar words are more understandable than longer, more complex, and less familiar words.

Use shorter and simpler sentences and phrases.

Use short sentences with simple grammatical structure. Shorten long sentences by removing unnecessary words or breaking them into two or more sentences. We should avoid complex phrases. For example, instead of using the phrase, "in the event of," replace it with "if."

Sentences longer than 15 to 20 words require more mental effort to understand. The reader must piece together concepts from the early part of the sentence with the later part. Review longer sentences and either make them shorter or split them into multiple sentences. Rewrite as needed for increased clarity.

Avoid passive voice.

Passive voice is more difficult to understand and often results in longer sentences. Use active voice instead. Here's an example of passive voice: "The correct answer should be circled." Instead, use active voice, "Circle the correct answer." Instructional writers should primarily use active voice because it's easier to understand and more concise.

Avoid negation.

Sentences with negative wording are more difficult to understand. Instead, use positive wording. For example, use, "Which of the following is" rather than, "Which of the following isn't."

Don't be wordy.

"In this section, you will be making a variety of important decisions about applying the policy change using various realistic situations you are likely to face" [26 words]. A more concise rewrite: "In this section, apply the policy change to a variety of realistic situations" [13 words].

I'm wordy by nature. That means I need to edit my text to be as concise as possible without losing meaning. I usually can't see all the wordiness, so an editor makes my words more concise still.

Avoid abstract language.

Abstract language is often unclear. Instead, use concrete and descriptive wording.

Abstract: "You will have greater success if you rest before the test."

Concrete: "Get a good night's sleep and eat a healthy breakfast before the test."

Improve readability.

Shrock & Coscarelli (2007) recommend we test the readability of assessments. Readability measures how easy (or difficult) it is to read a piece of text. Readability typically measures the complexity of text using syllables and sentence lengths. Microsoft Word can test readability, which is helpful if this is the application you use to write. The following image shows how I turn this feature on. (This may look different in your version of Word.) There are also many online readability apps.

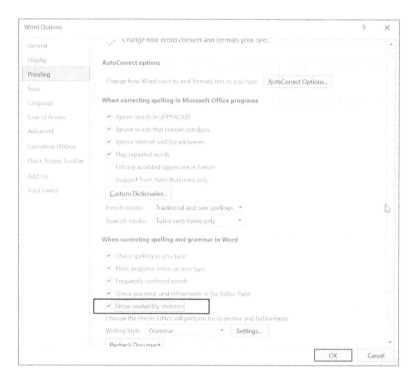

Checkbox for readability in Word Options in Microsoft Word

> Improving readability doesn't "dumb down" your assessment. It makes it easier for people to understand and demonstrate achievement of the learning objectives.

When readability is too low, we are often testing reading comprehension instead of the learning objectives. We can avoid this problem by checking readability and fixing it as needed.

Recently, I was excited to finally start reading a nonfiction book I'd bought after hearing the author speak. After two pages, I closed the book and I doubt I'll ever open it again. The writing was extremely challenging. Most people who know me would think I could read such a book. But here's the aha—I don't want to work that hard to understand. Your readers (including people with advanced degrees, according to research) don't want to work that hard, either. Make it easier.

Periods (and other punctuation) can make sentences easier or harder to understand. To make writing easier to read, be careful with punctuation.

If the stem is a question:
1. Each answer choice should end with a period if it is a complete sentence.
2. Each answer choice should not end with a period if it is a phrase.
3. If the answer choices are complete sentences, we should correctly capitalize and punctuate them.

If the stem is an incomplete sentence:
1. Each answer choice should complete the sentence.
2. Because each answer completes the sentence, it should end with a period.

Next are examples of punctuation where the stem is a question, and where it is an incomplete sentence.

If the stem is a question:	If the stem is an incomplete sentence:
How often do you need to replace the batteries in your smoke alarm? (Select the best answer.)	You need to replace the batteries in your smoke alarm every: (Select the best answer.)
a) Every six months	a) Six months.
a) Every year	a) Year.
b) Every two years	b) Two years.
All answer choices are phrases, so they don't end with a period.	Answer choices each complete the stem (an incomplete sentence), so each choice ends with a period.

I capitalize the beginning of all answer choices. There wasn't any guidance about this when I consulted the research. Next, I consulted three of my favorite academic books on writing test questions. None of them discussed the issue.

So, here's what I did. I looked to see how the author of each book capitalized their example multiple-choice questions. *Criterion-Referenced Test Development* (Shrock & Coscarelli, 2007), capitalizes the beginning of each answer choice. The other two do not. What should you do? Choose a way and then be consistent.

MORE...

Additional resources to improve understanding:
* Hemingway App
  Identifies common writing errors and calculates the reading level of your text
* Plain Language
  United States government resources for writing clearly and concisely. You can search for plain language resources available by other country government agencies as well.
* Shank, P. (2017). Write and Organize for Deeper Learning
  This book includes my tactics for better instructional writing, including readability.

To maintain the URLs more easily for online resources, they are available here: https://www.pattishank.com/mcqresources

Inclusive and Accessible Tests

I met Prakhar Jain, a learning designer from Adelaide, Australia, in one of my recent webinars. We shared insights about the importance of web accessibility, in general, and test accessibility specifically. In our view, people who design online instruction, including tests, have an ethical responsibility to make them accessible to a wide diversity of user experiences. I asked him to add some insights in this section and his insights are woven in with mine, so consider this section a joint effort. (Thank you, Prakhar!)

We often use test results to measure participants' success in a course or other instructional effort. There are many reasons people may experience difficulties managing typical testing conditions. These difficulties may be permanent, temporary, or situational.

We certainly don't want to make it hard for people to show they have met the objectives of the course. So, we must make our assessments work for the wider diversity of user experiences. This is critical because these problems are common rather than (as some test developers imagine) infrequent.

For example, someone may not have use of a hand (permanent). Another person may have a repetitive strain injury and their hand is unusable for months (temporary). Someone filing reports in their car may be using a laptop without a mouse (situational). There are many, many other examples.

Some of the most well-known difficulties include vision problems, hearing problems, mobility difficulties, functional limitations, cognitive limitations, communication limitations, test anxiety, and so on. Whether we realize it or not, at any given time, a significant portion of our participants deal with these and related issues.

In recent years, great strides have been made in ensuring diversity, inclusion, and accurate representation in all types of learning. Often, however, this broader definition may inadvertently exclude people who have permanent, temporary, or situational disabilities.

Accessibility is an important guideline in test design and should be implemented from the start. We must ensure that test content is compliant with keyboard and screen reader use. Accessibility involves intentional decisions to support the wide range of user experiences.

To be navigable and understood by a wide diversity of users, we should eliminate or reduce technology barriers. This makes technologies easier to use for all, including people who have disabilities.

For example, when texting, I (Patti) find it hard to use the tiny digital keyboard to type accurately, so I spend time correcting mistakes—which is even harder than typing. Instead, I use my phone's speech-to-text function that types what I say. Much faster and easier. This technology was originally developed for people with visual impairments. But it helps a wide diversity of people, including me.

Tactics to improve test accessibility are beyond the scope of this book but we urge you to learn more. Making tests accessible removes barriers from learning. It makes your test design and navigation simpler and more intuitive, speeds up loading times, and ensures greater compatibility with different devices and browsing platforms. It makes testing easier for all.

MORE...

Some good resources on inclusive and accessible design:
- Microsoft Inclusive Design
- Web Content Accessibility Guidelines (WCAG)
- WebAIM Design Resources
- Recordings from the Accessible and Inclusive Design Conference 2021
- Miller, S. (2021). Designing Accessible Learning Content. New York: Kogan Page Inc.

To maintain the URLs more easily for online resources, they are available here: https://www.pattishank.com/mcqresources

Item-Writing Flaws

Item flaws are violations of evidence-based guidelines for writing multiple-choice questions. The problem with item flaws is they introduce irrelevant difficulty. We want each item's difficulty to come from the knowledge and skills needed, not from how we write the item. We should avoid item flaws because they negatively affect an assessment's:
- Fairness, as flaws can change who passes or fails. People who know the content may not pass, while people who don't know the content could. Flaws can cause assessments to measure the wrong things. Not good!
- Reliability, as flaws can affect the consistency of the results.
- Validity, as flaws can reduce the ability of questions to measure important knowledge and skills.

Nedeau-Cayo's (2013) study on multiple-choice questions in a nursing certification exam showed that, of approximately 2,500 questions, 85% had at least one flaw—and about a third had two or more flaws. As this research and others show, flaws are commonplace. Since they can damage assessments, we must eliminate them.

The following are commonly cited item flaws. I discussed many of these earlier and am reviewing some of the most damaging flaws as a reminder to not make them!

Common Question Flaws

Lack of alignment with the learning objective	Questions must measure important knowledge and skills embedded in the learning objective.

Common Stem Flaws

Incomplete	The stem should present a clear question that is understandable without reading the answer choices.
Necessary/unnecessary details	The stem should include all details needed to answer the question. In most cases, it should not include unnecessary details, as this is confusing and increases the amount of time needed to answer.
Negatively phrased	When we phrase the stem negatively, participants often misinterpret it—leading to incorrect answers even when they know the correct answer. Use positive phrasing instead. When we can't avoid negative phrasing, bold or capitalize the phrase or words. This helps only a bit, so negative phrasing should be rare.

Common Alternative Answer Flaws

Same position for the correct answer	Multiple-choice question writers may unintentionally put correct answers in the same answer choice position. Be sure to intentionally move the position of the correct answer so the correct answer position isn't easy to guess.

All of the above, none of the above, and answers that combine answers	Avoid these answer choices, as they perform poorly. When multiple answers are needed to assess the learning objective, consider the multiple-correct question format.
Implausible distractors	Write all incorrect answers so they are plausible to people who do not have the needed knowledge and skills.
No unambiguously correct or best answer	Make sure the correct answer is unambiguously correct or best to someone with the needed knowledge.
One answer choice longer than others	Write all the answer choices so they are the same length and depth.

Next are three examples of flawed questions and how to fix them.

Example 1

Which of the following should not be used to smother a grease fire in a pan on the stove? (Select the best answer.)
1. A metal lid
2. Water *
3. A Class B fire extinguisher

The stem is negatively stated, which makes it harder to understand. Better stem: What is the problem with using water to smother a grease fire on the stove?

Example 2

A medication side effect is: (Select the correct answer.)
a) An unapproved or unofficial usage of the medication.
b) An unintended symptom from using the medication. *
c) A medical problem occurring on the side of the body.

Answer c is not plausible. Better answer choice for c: An intermittent problem that is hard to diagnose.

Example 3

Which of the following is rarely true? (Select the correct answer.)
a)   Hydroponics have bigger yields than growing in soils.
b)   Hydroponics grow faster than growing in soils.
c)   Hydroponics take up less space than growing in soils.
d)   Hydroponics save water as compared to growing in soils.
e)   None of the above *

The stem is negatively worded and incomplete. None of the above should not be used as an answer choice. Better stem: Which of the following are benefits of hydroponic gardening? (Select the two correct answers.)

When You Aren't the Content Expert

You may be asked to write assessment questions when you aren't an expert in the domain being assessed. You might be an instructional designer, instructional developer, writer, or have a different title. You might work in a company, academia, or elsewhere.

Regardless of your title or organization, if you have little or no experience in the domain, it's difficult to know the outcomes needed from instruction and how to assess those outcomes. You'll need to work with and rely on people more expert in the areas being assessed. Here are two of my work situations and the insights I gained about writing assessment questions with and for them.

I worked with an organization producing complex software for highly specialized, scientific analysis. The scientists who developed the software needed to train people to perform complex and specialized tasks. Previous attempts at training had been unsuccessful—causing headaches for their organization.

I didn't have the background knowledge to learn these tasks in a reasonable amount of time. I could, however, understand the thought processes (mostly analysis) they needed to assess and match them with proper assessment methods. We decided to train and assess users through scenarios—from less complex to more complex. We added questions to assess whether they understood what they were doing and why.

In a different situation, I worked with an organization training non-technical leaders in advanced technologies. They needed help writing multiple-choice questions to assess what they taught. I had some background knowledge, but I worked with their experts because I wasn't one.

The primary assessment goal was to see whether participants understood how the technologies worked and the impact they were having. I made the first attempt at writing questions. They selected the most appropriate ones. They fixed wording that wasn't precise enough and reworded distractors to make them more plausible to their participants.

Over time, they learned what they needed to know to write the questions. Initially, I continued to fix their questions to follow question-writing guidelines. Over time, they needed less of my help, which was one of our desired outcomes.

I've learned a lot about working with experts to design valuable and valid instruction and multiple-choice questions in my work. In many cases, experts are busy and often don't have time to take courses to become good multiple-choice question writers. But their questions do have to be well written.

Helping experts become better question writers means being good question writing partners. This varies based on the situation you are in, but there are commonalities. Like, if the content is unknown to you or too complex, you can't write their questions on your own. If you do, the questions are likely to be too low level, even if well written. A well-written question is still ineffective if it measures the wrong thing.

Here are guidelines I use when working with experts to build multiple-choice questions.

- Respect their time and needs. Learn their constraints (time is a common limitation) and how they can best work with you.
- Create a schedule and plan that meets their needs. Expect schedule changes because, like you, their priorities shift and they need to respond to them.
- Whenever possible, work with a *group* of more expert people, not just one person. Guy Wallace helped me understand that a single person is likely to miss important things. Others being involved helps uncover things that would otherwise go missing. I have found a group of more expert people to be more engaged than a single person because they get to see others' insights. They often like editing each other's questions, too.
- Have evidence-based guidelines at hand for dealing with questions and objections. I especially like Haladyna's *Developing and Validating Multiple-Choice Test Items*, 3rd Edition for this purpose. This book's Chapter 5 discusses these guidelines in detail.
- Supply a process for writing good questions. Next is a template I use to understand real-life and job-task assessment needs when working with content experts.

Complete for each task.

Task:

_____

Who does this task?

_____

What do they need to be able to do? When? Under what circumstances? Using what tools and resources?

_____

What important decisions are made when doing the task?

_____

How will we know if they perform satisfactorily?

_____

What are common and important situations where they perform this task?

_____

What are common misunderstandings less experienced people have when doing this task? What problems do these misunderstandings cause?

_____

How frequently is this task done?
Extremely frequently   Frequently   Not very frequently   Rarely

How important are the task results?
Extremely important   Important   Less important   Not important

Many of the questions in the template ask about the ABCDs of the learning objective, which describes what needs to be assessed. The common situations and common decisions questions inform good stems. The common misunderstandings inform plausible distractors. And the last two questions help you prioritize what needs to be assessed.

Helping experts write better questions is important. I'd like to offer the best advice I can. Please reach out with other tactics that work for you so I can add them in future versions of this book.

LEARNING OBJECTIVES AND MULTIPLE-CHOICE QUESTION GUIDELINES

Learning objectives
- [ ] Create learning objectives that describe important real-life or job knowledge and skills.
- [ ] State who performs the task (A), what the performer is doing (B), the context of performance—when, under what circumstances, using what knowledge, resources, or tools (C), and how we can tell if performance meets the standard (D).

Assessment content
- [ ] Assess important knowledge and skills embedded in the learning objective.
- [ ] Assess central, critical content rather than less-important content.
- [ ] Use correct grammar, spelling, and punctuation.
- [ ] Use clear, concise, easily understood, and non-ambiguous wording.
- [ ] Avoid negatives and double negatives.
- [ ] Avoid trick questions.
- [ ] Avoid these terms: always, often, frequently, never, none, rarely, and infrequently.

Stem
- [ ] Make the stem as concise as possible.
- [ ] Provide enough information so what is being tested is clear without reading the answers.
- [ ] Use a question or incomplete sentence.
- [ ] Use simple rather than complex wording and shorter sentences.
- [ ] Use concise problems and situations as appropriate.
- [ ] Don't supply unnecessary information or irrelevant sources of difficulty.
- [ ] Use appropriate media when the actual task requires viewing or listening.
- [ ] Avoid negative wording.
- [ ] Use "should" instead of "could."
- [ ] Offer no clues as to the correct answer.

Answers

- ☐ Three answer choices are usually ideal. You can use more or vary the number of distractors when ALL distractors are plausible.
- ☐ Make answer choices as concise as possible.
- ☐ Keep all answers about the same length and depth.
- ☐ Write answers that are clear, unambiguous, grammatically correct, and punctuated correctly.
- ☐ Use parallel construction ("using," "placing," "making").
- ☐ When answers provide best and less-optimal alternatives (Select the best answer), provide enough detail to distinguish best from less good.
- ☐ Avoid answer choices that combine answers ("b and c").
- ☐ Avoid "all of the above" and "none of the above."
- ☐ Arrange answers in logical order: date, number, degree, order, etc.
- ☐ Avoid highly technical or jargony answers unless assessing technical knowledge and jargon.
- ☐ Offer no clues as to the correct answer.

Key

- ☐ Make the key clearly and correctly answer the question or incomplete sentence.
- ☐ Make the key unambiguously correct to those with the needed knowledge and skill.
- ☐ Use different placements of the key.

Distractors

- ☐ Make sure distractors are incorrect or not best to those with the needed knowledge and skill.
- ☐ Make distractors plausible to those without the needed knowledge and skill. The best plausible-but-incorrect distractors are:
  - – Misconceptions and errors in thinking for people without the needed knowledge.
  - – Correct content paraphrased incorrectly.
- ☐ Don't use implausible distractors.

Instructions

☐ Provide clear instructions for the assessment and for groups of questions. May include:
  - How the question is scored (e.g., do grammar and spelling errors count?)
  - Whether answers can be changed
  - Time constraints
  - Tools and resources needed, available, not permitted
  - How to select correct answers (e.g., click a box, drag the answer, type an answer, etc.)

☐ State whether test takers should select the correct answer, best answer, or multiple answers.
  - For a question with one correct answer, ask for the correct answer. (Select the correct answer.)
  - For a question with one best answer, ask for the best answer. (Select the best answer.)
  - For a question with more than one correct answer, ask for the number of correct answers. (Select the X correct answers.)

Exercise Answers

Exercise 3-1. For the two learning objectives shown (left column), write a stem that assesses important knowledge and skills.

Learning Objective	Stem
Students will calculate the mean score from a series of test scores.	Calculate the mean score from the following test scores.
Technicians will select the appropriate personal protective equipment for a given pesticide application situation.	You want to use diatomaceous earth to kill the ants in your kitchen. What personal protective equipment should you put on before applying this treatment?

Exercise 3-2. For the stem and correct answer below, write an incorrectly paraphrased distractor.

Stem:
You are inputting a new vendor into the vendor database. You are in a hurry and don't add the vendor's address. Which of the following is an important consequence of not inputting the vendor address information at the time of vendor setup? (Select the best answer.)

Correct answer:
The vendor will not appear in regional sales reports.

My distractor:
The vendor will not receive notice of account setup.

Your distractor? (There are many possible answers. Here are a few.)
The vendor will be on conditional status for 30 days.
The vendor will not receive refunds on returned items.

Exercise 3-3. For the two correct answers shown (left column), write a distractor that incorrectly paraphrases the correct answer.

Correct answer	Distractors
A fire extinguisher rated for grease fires.	A fire extinguisher rated for paper fires.
Replace with a part with the exact same part number.	Replace with a part in the same series number.
30 days after enrolling	45 days after enrolling

Chapter Insights

Stem
- The two best formats for a stem are a question and an incomplete sentence. Researchers consider an incomplete sentence somewhat harder to understand than a question.

Answer Choices
- Answer choices include the correct answer (key) and the incorrect answers (distractors).
- Good distractors are plausible to those who do not know the content being tested. Bad distractors help those who don't know the content to eliminate those choices and make guessing easier.
- Research suggests creating distractors from common misconceptions and errors in thinking, and from paraphrasing the correct answer.
- All answer choices for a specific question should be of similar length and depth.
- Three answer choices typically perform as well or better than additional answer choices.

Item Flaws
- Item flaws are violations of evidence-based guidelines for writing multiple-choice questions.
- Common item flaws include lack of alignment between the question and the learning objective, incomplete stems, unnecessary details in the stem, stems phrased negatively, reusing the same position for the correct answer, the longest answer being correct, using all of the above and none of the above as answer choices, writing implausible distractors, and not having an unambiguously correct answer.

Understanding
- We cannot assess the knowledge and skills in the learning objective if participants have difficulties understanding the instructions or the questions! Some comprehension issues to address include long and complex wording or phrases, passive voice, negative phrasing, long sentences, being too wordy, and using abstract language. We also need to punctuate questions correctly.

- We should test the readability of our assessments so we can make them easier to read. When readability is too low, we are often testing reading comprehension rather than the learning objectives.

Inclusive and Accessible Tests

- There are many reasons people experience problems successfully managing typical testing conditions. Because these problems are common and we certainly don't want to make it hard for people to show that they have met the objectives, we need to make accommodations and create accessible tests.

Chapter References

Abedi, J. (2006). Language Issues in Item Development. In S. M. Downing & T. M. Haladyna (Eds.), Handbook of test development (p. 377–398). Lawrence Erlbaum Associates Publishers.

Badgett, B. A. (2010). Toward the development of a model to estimate the readability of credentialing examination materials. UNLV Theses, Dissertations, Professional Papers, and Capstones.

Butler, A. C. (2018). Multiple-choice testing in education: Are the best practices for assessment also good for learning? Journal of Applied Research in Memory and Cognition, 7(3), 323-331.

Burton, S. J., Sudweeks, R. R., Merrill, P. F., & Wood, B. (1991). How to prepare better multiple-choice test items: guidelines for university faculty. Brigham Young University Testing Services and The Department of Instructional Science.

Case, S. M. & Downing, S. M. (1989). Performance of various multiple-choice item types on medical specialty examinations: Types A, B, C, K, and X. Proceedings of the Twenty-Eighth Annual Conference on Research in Medical Education, pp. 167–172.

Case, S. M. & Swanson, D. B. (2001). Constructing written test questions for the basic and clinical sciences (2nd Ed.). Philadelphia, PA: National Board of Medical Examiners.

Chiavaroli, N. (2017). Negatively-worded multiple choice questions: An avoidable threat to validity. Practical Assessment, Research & Evaluation, 22(3), 1-14.

Collins, J. (2006). Writing multiple-choice questions for continuing medical education activities and self-assessment modules. Radiographics 26, 543–551.

Downing, S. M. (2005). The effects of violating standard item writing principles on tests and students: the consequences of using flawed test items on achievement examinations in medical education. Advances in Health Sciences Education, 10, 133–143.

Dragan, M. & Woo, A. The methodology used to assess the readability of the NNAAP™ examination. National Council of the State Boards of Nursing. NNAAP™ and MACE™ Technical Brief.

Frisbie, D. A. (1990). The evolution of the multiple true-false item format. Paper presented at the Annual Meeting of the National Council on Measurement in Education, Boston.

Frisbie, D. A. (1992). The multiple true-false item format: A status review. Educational Measurement: Issues and Practice, 5(4), 21–26.

Frisbie, D. A. (1992). The status of multiple true-false testing. Educational Measurement: Issues and Practices, 5, 21-26.

Frisbie, D. A. & Becker, D. F. (1991). An analysis of textbook advice about true-false tests. Applied Measurement in Education, 4, 67–83.

Gierl, M. J., Bulut, O., Guo, Q., & Zhang, X. (2017). Developing, analyzing, and using distractors for multiple-choice tests in education: A comprehensive review. Review of Educational Research, 87: 6, pp. 1082–1116.

Haladyna, T. M. (1997). Writing test items to evaluate higher order thinking skills. Needham Heights, MA: Allyn and Bacon.

Haladyna, T. M. (2004). Developing and validating multiple-choice test items. Mahwah, NJ: Lawrence Erlbaum Associates, Inc.

Haladyna, T. M. & Downing, S. M. (1989). A taxonomy of multiple-choice item-writing rules. Applied Measurement in Education, 1, 37–50.

Haladyna, T. M. & Downing, S. M. (1988). Functional distractors: Implications for test-item writing and test design. Paper presented at the annual meeting of the American Educational Research Association, New Orleans, Louisiana.

Haladyna, T. M. & Downing, S. M. (1989). A taxonomy of multiple-choice item-writing rules. Applied Measurement in Education, 2(1), 37-50.

Haladyna, T. M. & Downing, S. M. (1989). The validity of a taxonomy of multiple-choice item-writing rules. Applied Measurement in Education, 1, 51–78.

Haladyna, T. M. & Downing, S. M. (1993). How many options is enough for a multiple-choice test item? Educational and Psychological Measurement, 999–1010.

Haladyna, T. M., Downing, S. M., Rodriguez, M. (2002.) A review of multiple-choice item-writing guidelines for classroom assessment. Applied Measurement in Education, 15, 309–34.

Haladyna, T. M. & Rodriguez, M. (2013). Developing and validating test items. New York: Routledge.

Haladyna, T. M., Rodriguez, M. C., & Stevens, C. (2019) Are multiple-choice items too fat? Applied Measurement in Education, 32:4, 350-364.

Lai, H., Gierl, M. J., Touchie, C., Pugh, D., Boulais, A., & De Champlain, A. (2016). Using automatic item generation to improve the quality of MCQ distractors. Teaching and Learning in Medicine, 28, 166–173.

Linn, R. & Miller, M. (2005). Measurement and assessment in teaching (9th ed.). Upper Saddle River, N.J.: Prentice Hall.

Little, J. L., Bjork, E. L., Bjork, R. A., & Angello, G. (2012). Multiple-choice tests exonerated, at least of some charges: Fostering test-induced learning and avoiding test-induced forgetting. Psychological Science, 23, 1337-1344.

Marelli, A. E. (1995). Writing multiple-choice test items. Performance and Instruction, 34(8), 24–29.

Marsh, E. J. & Cantor, A. D. (2014). Chapter 02: Learning from the test: Dos and don'ts for using multiple-choice tests, in McDaniel, M. A., Frey, R. F., Fitzpatrick, S. M., & Roediger, H. L. (Eds.), Integrating Cognitive Science with Innovative Teaching in STEM Disciplines. Washington University, Saint Louis, Missouri.

Marzano, R. J., Brandt, R. S., Hughes, C. S., Jones, B. F., Presseisen, B. Z, Ranking, S. C., & Suhor, C. (1988). Dimensions of thinking: A framework for curriculum and instruction. Alexandria, VA: Association for Supervision and Curriculum Development.

Nedeau-Cayo, R., Laughlin, D., Rus, L., & Hall, J. (2013). Assessment of item-writing flaws in multiple-choice questions. Journal for Nurses in Professional Development, 29, 52–57.

Rauschert, E. S. J., Yang, S. M., & Pigg, R. M. (2018). Which of the following is true: We can write better multiple choice questions. Bulletin of the Ecological Society of America 100(1).

Rodriguez, M. C. (2005). Three options are optimal for multiple-choice items: A meta-analysis of 80 years of research. Educational Measurement Issues and Practice, 24(2), 3–13.

Roediger, H. L., III, & Marsh, E. J. (2005). The positive and negative consequences of multiple-choice testing. Journal of Experimental Psychology: Learning, Memory, and Cognition, 31, 1155-1159.

Rohrer, D., Taylor, K., & Sholar, B. (2010). Tests enhance the transfer of learning. Journal of Experimental Psychology: Learning, Memory, and Cognition, 36, 233-239.

Schuwirth, L. W. T. & van der Vleuten, C. P. M. (2004). Different written assessment methods: what can be said about their strengths and weaknesses? Medical Education, 38, 974–979.

Shin, J., Guo, Q. &, Gierl, M. J. (2019). Multiple-choice item distractor development using topic modeling approaches. Frontiers in Psychology, 10.

Shrock, S. A. & Coscarelli, W. C. (1998). Make the test match the job. Quality.

Shrock, S. A. & Coscarelli, W. C. (2007). Criterion-referenced test development: Technical and legal guidelines for corporate training and certification (3rd ed.). Silver Spring: Pfeiffer.

Statman, S. (1988). Ask a clear question and get a clear answer: An enquiry into the question/answer and the sentence completion formats of multiple-choice items. System, 16, 367–376.

Sudman, S., Bradburn, N. M., & Schwarz, N. (1996). Thinking about answers: The application of cognitive processes to survey methodology. Jossey-Bass.

Sugrue, B. (2002). Problems with Bloom's taxonomy.

Sugrue, B. (2013). A learning science alternative to Bloom's taxonomy. Learning Solutions Magazine.

Tarrant, M., & Ware, J. (2008). Impact of item-writing flaws in multiple-choice questions on student achievement in high-stakes nursing assessments. Medical Education, 42, 198–206.

Tarrant, M., Knierim, A., Hayes, S. K., & Ware, J. (2006). The frequency of item writing flaws in multiple-choice questions used in high stakes nursing assessments. Nurse Education Today, 26, 662–671.

Vyas, R. (2008). Multiple choice questions: A literature review on the optimal number of options. Medical education. The National Medical Journal of India, 21(3).

Zimmerman, B. B., Sudweeks, R. R., Shelley, M. F., & Wood, B. (1990). How to Prepare Better Tests: Guidelines for University Faculty. Provo, UT: Brigham Young University Testing Services.

Chapter 4:
Higher-Level Questions

In this chapter, I discuss how to better assess *important* knowledge and skills in learning objectives. The image below shows three levels of thinking. The two outer circles align with many of the thought processes we want to assess with multiple-choice questions (Sugrue, 2002; Haladyna, 1997; Haladyna & Rodriguez, 2013). It is the sweet spot for the most relevant multiple-choice questions.

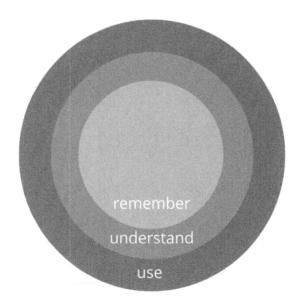

These levels represent:
- **Remember:** What we recall or recognize
- **Understand:** What we understand
- **Use:** The ability to use what we remember and understand to perform complex real-life and job tasks

The single most important way to improve assessments is to test above the remember level (Shrock & Coscarelli, 2007). The thought processes we want to prompt during assessment are the same thought processes that participants use when they are doing the task in real life or on the job (Berk, 1997). In other words, what people need to be able to do is what we should assess.

If, in real life or on the job, people must be able to:	*then*	During assessment, we should assess whether they can:
Make sense of data.		Make sense of data.
Analyze which rules apply.		Analyze which rules apply.
Evaluate what could go wrong.		Evaluate what could go wrong.
Decide which step to take next.		Decide which step to take next.

TRY THIS!

Exercise 4-1. For the two learning objectives shown (left column), describe what we should assess (right column).

I completed the first item to show you how to do the exercise.

Exercise answers are at the end of this chapter. You will learn more if you do the exercise *before* you review the answers.

Task	What should we assess?
Students will calculate the mean from a series of numbers.	Calculate the mean score from the following test scores.
Homeowners will select the appropriate personal protective equipment before applying pesticides and other pest treatments.	
Couples will make good decisions about using credit in a variety of situations.	

Thought Processes

Recall that we primarily want to assess the understand and use levels, as shown in the image below.

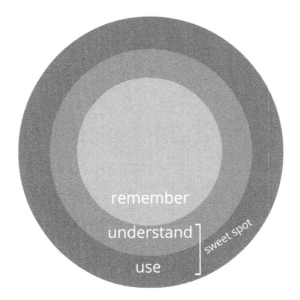

Assessing **understanding** typically asks test takers to select correct definitions, examples, and characteristics. Here are three examples of multiple-choice questions that assess understanding.

Example 1

What is Samina assessing when she reconciles her cash drawer at the end of each shift? (Select the best answer.)

Example 2

What does the code in the example show?

```
<ul>
  <li>Hot coffee</li>
  <li>Hot tea</li>
  <li>Iced coffee</li>

  <li>Iced tea</li>
</ul>
```

Example 3

You're working in the produce department and a customer asks if this pepper is organic. The following PLU code sticker is on the fruit. What do you tell the customer?

When we write questions about definitions and characteristics, we should ideally paraphrase the instructional content. Asking test takers to select the exact definition or characteristic from the content is a remember task. Likewise, examples used in questions should be new examples, as asking people to select the examples from the content is a remember task.

Assessing **use** typically asks test takers to apply what they remember and understand to perform complex real life and job tasks. Haladyna (1997) discusses these common types of use: evaluating, problem solving, and predicting.

Evaluating means judging and making choices based on those judgments. Many work tasks require this thought process. For example, there are many times at work when we evaluate which approach will work best.

Here are three examples of multiple-choice questions that assess evaluating.

Example 1

[Diagram] Which of the cables shown will connect this monitor to this laptop computer?

Example 2

Marcus has been on staff for two months and arrived 20 minutes late for work today. This is the first time he has been late for work, and he was late because his car wouldn't start. Based on the tardiness policy, what should you do?

Example 3

Your insurance plan has a yearly deductible of $4,000 before it pays for approved medical expenses. In a calendar year, once you pay the deductible, your plan pays 80% of approved medical expenses through the end of the year. If your first approved medical expense during the year is $5,025, how much of this expense will the plan pay?

Problem solving means taking steps that lead to a solution. It involves identifying the problem, analyzing the problem, proposing solutions, testing solutions, and drawing conclusions.

Here are two examples of multiple-choice questions that assess problem solving.

Example 1

The SN620 document shredder has stopped shredding paper. The red light next to the paper feed is on. What is the fix for this problem?

Example 2

Jean works in the produce department of a large grocery store. When she arrives at work, she sees that apples recently arrived. The Fuji apples are much smaller than usual. What should Jean do next?

Predicting means forecasting specific outcomes. For example, we often need to predict the results of actions we might take. Accurate prediction involves recognizing relationships between actions or events and probable results.

Here are three examples of multiple-choice questions that assess predicting.

Example 1

Ana tests her blood sugar. It is 65 mg/dl. What other symptoms is she likely to have?

Example 2

[audio clip] Damien tries to start his car and hears this sound. The sound indicates which of the following parts may not be operational?

Example 3

[image] This item arrived in the condition shown. What is the likely cause of this damage?

This table lists these thought processes and shows typical stems for each one.

Thinking type		Typical stems
Understanding:	Definitions	What is the definition...
	Characteristics	Which is characteristic of...
	Examples	Which is an example of...
Evaluating:	Criteria	Which criteria should we use...
	Use criteria to evaluate	What is the most effective...
		Which is the best/worst...
Problem solving:	Identify the problem	What is the problem...
		What information is needed...
	Analyze the problem	What would you conclude from...
	Propose solution(s)	What is the first/next step...
	Test solutions	Which solution is best...
	Draw conclusions	What conclusions can you draw...
Predicting:	Cause	What is the cause...
	Effect	What will happen if...

TRY THIS!

Exercise 4-2. Using the learning objective below, write a stem for relevant thought processes.

I completed the first item to show you how to do the exercise.

Exercise answers are at the end of this chapter. You will learn more if you do the exercise *before* you review the answers.

LO: The cashier will calculate the correct change based on total purchase paid in cash.

Thought Process	Stem
Understanding	What does "correct change" mean?
Evaluating	

Use What You Remember

A simple way to test beyond the remember level is to ask people to *use* what they remember. For example, here's a learning objective:

Web designers will create ordered and unordered HTML lists.

The following question is written at the remember level and assesses whether test takers remember that <li> tags indicate list items.

What does the <li> HTML element indicate?
   a)   Line break
   b)   List item *
   c)   Link

In the following example, the test taker must *use* what they remember about HTML lists to interpret the HTML code. Interpreting requires higher-level thought processes.

What does the following HTML code indicate? (Select the correct answer.)
```
<ol>
   <li>5x7</li>
   <li>5x8</li>
   <li>7x10</li>
   <li>8x10</li>
</ol>
```
   a)   four numbered list items *
   b)   four description list items
   c)   four bulleted list items

Asking participants to use what they remember helps us create higher-level questions. Here's another example.

Student lab assistants will monitor and manage the safety of people, chemicals, and equipment while assisting with laboratory experiments.

Below are two potential questions to assess this learning objective. The top question asks test takers to remember course material. The bottom question asks test takers to use what they remember.

Where should we secure personal items such as coats, purses, and books before experiments begin? (Remember)

Josie and Elena are set up for today's experiment. Josie was late to class and threw her purse and phone on an unused station chair. When can they start the experiment? (Use what you remember)

A common variation of the use-what-you-remember question is use-what-you-look-up questions. These questions ask test takers to find and use documentation to answer relevant and realistic questions. I especially like use-what-you-look-up questions when the task requires use of specific documents such as guidelines, reference materials, or a checklist that are not expected to be memorized.

> Poorly-written multiple-choice questions commonly ask people to recall content they don't need to recall in real life. We want to assess the thinking used in the real task. Consider use-what-you-look-up questions to assess whether participants can find needed information and use it as they should in the real world.

The following shows a use-what-you-look-up stem for the same learning objective.

When working with tissue cultures in the laboratory, what should we do to protect participants from spills?
BCA Lab Safety Manual.

In this question, test takers use the link to find the answer in the actual reference document. If a task requires looking up information in documentation, it makes sense to assess whether participants can find needed information in that documentation.

You may have noticed that quite a few of my questions include situations. A stem that describes a situation should concentrate on important situations that participants are likely to face in real life or on the job. These situations typically include relevant details for making decisions. They may also include media to "show" and "tell," which can make questions like the real task.

The following are characteristics of a good situation.

Plausible
Write situations that are realistic and plausible. They should require participants to respond as they would in real life or on the job.

Concise
Write situations that are clear and include only needed information.

Includes needed details
Include all details needed to answer the question. We should avoid unnecessary details—especially with less-proficient participants.

We may add extra details when the learning objective requires distinguishing between necessary information and unnecessary information. These are usually used with more proficient participants.

Occurs in the present
For ease of understanding, write most situations in present tense. Past or future tense are acceptable to describe events that happened in the past or that we expect to occur in the future.

Next is an example of a situation question with two multiple-choice questions.

The Daily Grub Restaurant kitchen has regular inspections from food inspectors. In an inspection a week ago, the inspector wrote two violations. One was for not storing meat in the correct place in the refrigerator and the other was for baked potatoes left out without refrigeration.

Where should we store meat in the refrigerator until cooked?
- a) In the coldest place
- b) On the top shelf
- c) On the bottom shelf *

Can a restaurant leave baked potatoes out without refrigeration?
- a) Yes. In this case, the inspector made a mistake in writing this violation.
- b) No. They should cool them in the refrigerator if not used immediately. *
- c) It depends. They should be refrigerated once they reach 100° F.

Scenario research offers helpful insights for building better situation questions (Clark, 2013; Kanjilal et al., 2014). When writing situation questions we should:

1. Use the learning objective to select an important and realistic task that participants must perform adequately.
2. Add relevant context that helps test takers analyze which actions to take. Context may include location, time, people, constraints, information and resources, tools, and guidelines or rules.
3. Write the correct action for this situation in this context (correct answer).
4. Write common or plausible mistakes by people who have inadequate knowledge (distractors).

Here's an example of building a situation using these insights.

LO: Younger drivers will appropriately respond to weather-related driving situations.

Include	Situation Details
Use the learning objective to select an important and realistic task participants must perform adequately.	Teen driver, driving in the rain, and other drivers acting poorly
Add relevant context that helps knowledgeable participants analyze what actions to take. May include: location, time, people involved, constraints, information and resources, tools, and guidelines or rules.	Driving to a friend's house Raining hard Puddles from the rain Splashing, hard to see at times Annoyed tailgater driving behind
Write the correct action for this task in this context (correct answer).	Allow the annoyed tailgater to pass
Write common or plausible mistakes by people who have inadequate knowledge (distractors).	Drive at a safe speed Annoy the tailgater

Here's a multiple-choice question I built using these elements.

Angel, age 17, is driving to his friend's home in heavy rain. Some drivers are driving too fast, causing lots of splashing, which makes it hard to see. He is driving carefully but the car behind him is following close behind and honking the horn. How should he handle the situation? (Select the best answer.)

    a)   Pull over and let the other driver pass to reduce chances of an accident. *

    b)   Drive at a safe speed for the road conditions; ignore the driver behind.

    c)   Wave to the follower to acknowledge he wants to get around your car.

TRY THIS!

Exercise 4-3. Using the learning objective shown below, write a situation and a multiple-choice question.

I completed the first item to show you how to do the exercise.

Exercise answers are at the end of this chapter. You will learn more if you do the exercise *before* you review the answers.

LO: People who are currently renting an apartment will analyze whether they should continue to rent or buy a home.

Include	Situation Details
Use the learning objective to select an important and realistic task participants must perform adequately.	Decide whether to continue renting or buy a home using the home payment calculator.
Add relevant context that helps knowledgeable participants analyze what actions to take. May include: location, time, people involved, constraints, information and resources, tools, and guidelines or rules.	
Write the correct action for this task in this context (for the correct answer).	
Write common or plausible mistakes by people who have inadequate knowledge (for the distractors).	

Multiple-choice question:

Best Answer Questions

Question writers I work with are often unhappy about writing answer choices that could be construed as correct. They prefer to only use answer choices that are fully correct or fully incorrect so answer choices cannot "trick" the test takers.

There is an important reason we write distractors that could be construed as correct. The thinking process we need to assess requires test takers to distinguish between the best course of action, less-good courses of action, and bad courses of action.

Remember Berk (1997) telling us we need to assess in our questions the thought processes used while performing? I paraphrase this as, "What people need to do is what we should assess." Real-life and job tasks often require us to distinguish between the best (more optimal), less-good (less optimal), and bad (suboptimal) options. When people need to distinguish between best, less-good, and bad options in real life or on the job, it is fully appropriate to have them do this in multiple-choice questions.

Here's an example question that requires window covering sales people to distinguish between best, less-good, and bad options, just like on the job.

Katya wants to buy window coverings for her large, west-facing kitchen window. She says the current window coverings—3-inch wood blinds—make the kitchen seem dark, and she would like more light. She's worried about using window coverings that her two cats could easily damage and wants a more modern look. Which of the following window coverings best meets her needs? (Select the best answer.)
   a) Light-filtering double-cell honeycomb shades
   b) Woven wood shades without a muslin lining
   c) Vinyl vertical blinds that stack to the side *

> We want to know if test takers can select the best answer based on the circumstances, as they must do in real life.

In this case, the only answer choice that can let in a lot of light, is resistant to pet damage, and looks uncluttered is answer c. Answers a and b don't best meet her requirements.

Higher-level multiple-choice questions often require test takers to decide what is best because this is what they need to do in real life or on the job. As a result, many higher-level multiple-choice questions ask which answer choice is best (rather than correct). We are not tricking people when we ask them to select the best answer when this is what they must to do in real life or on the job.

Here's another example of a multiple-choice question where the distractors have elements of truth but are not the best answer for this question.

Johanna is feeling lightheaded and shaky and wants to test her blood sugar to see whether she is experiencing hypoglycemia (low blood sugar). What should she do first? (Select the best answer.)
  a) Gather the glucometer and supplies. *
  b) Replace the lancet in the lancing device.
  c) Review previous blood sugar readings.

The correct answer is a. There are certainly times where you might replace the lancet or review previous blood sugar readings before testing your blood sugar. Under these circumstances, a potential emergency, these plausible distractors are not best.

I hope I have convinced you that using questions that ask people to select the best answer is acceptable and often necessary.

What About Bloom's Taxonomy?

When teaching this content, participants repeatedly ask why I don't reference and use Bloom's Taxonomy (Bloom et al., 1956). Bloom wrote the *Taxonomy of Educational Objectives* before we understood more fully how cognition and learning work. There have been important insights since this time that better reflect thought processes.

There is a compelling article about problems with using Bloom's Taxonomy for objectives and assessment purposes. Sugrue explains that more recent taxonomies based on cognitive processes distinguish types of content and thought processes (Sugrue, 2002).

For many, Bloom's Taxonomy is instructional dogma. Still, it's worthwhile to reevaluate dogma from time to time considering recent evidence. A visual representation of my thinking about thought processes is at the beginning of this chapter. It was deeply informed by others' work (Sugrue, 2002, 2013; Berk, 1997; Haladyna, 1997, 2004).

More...

Brenda Sugrue's article on Bloom's Taxonomy:

Problems with Bloom's Taxonomy
A Learning Science Alternative to Bloom's Taxonomy

To maintain the URLs more easily for online resources, they are available here: https://www.pattishank.com/mcqresources

Exercise Answers

Exercise 4-1. For the two learning objectives shown (left column), describe what we should assess (right column).

Task	What should we assess?
Students will calculate the mean from a series of numbers.	Can they calculate the mean from the following test scores?
Homeowners will select the appropriate personal protective equipment before applying pesticides and other pest treatments.	Can they select the appropriate personal protective equipment before applying pesticides and other pest treatments?
Couples will make good decisions about using credit in a variety of situations.	Can they decide whether to use credit in a variety of situations?

Exercise 4-2. Using the learning objective below, write a stem for relevant thought processes.

LO: The cashier will calculate the correct change based on total purchases paid with cash.

Thought Process	Stem
Understanding	What does "correct change" mean?
Evaluating	How much change should you return if the buyer uses a $20 bill to pay for an item that costs $7.53 including tax?

Exercise 4-3. Using the learning objective shown below, write a situation and a multiple-choice question.

LO: People who are currently renting an apartment will analyze whether they should continue to rent or buy a home.

Include	Situation Details
Use the learning objective to select an important and realistic task participants must perform adequately.	Decide whether to continue renting or buy a home using the home payment calculator.
Add relevant context that helps knowledgeable participants analyze what actions to take. May include: location, time, people involved, constraints, information and resources, tools, and guidelines or rules.	Doug and Marissa live in an apartment but want to buy a home. Have saved $30,000 for a down payment. Current net income $5,735/month. Student loan debt $1,200/month, paid off in two more years
Write the correct action for this task in this context (for the correct answer).	Pay off the loan now, save for a down payment for two years and then buy. *
Write common or plausible mistakes by people who have inadequate knowledge (for the distractors).	Buy a home now and reduce the student loan payment to pay over five years. Buy a home in a year after paying down the student loan 60%.

Multiple-choice question:
Doug and Marissa live in an apartment and want to buy a home. They have saved $15,000 for a down payment. Their current net income is $5,735 per month, and they are debt-free except for a student loan of $1,200/month. With the current payments, the student loan will be paid off in two years. Using the home payment calculator, when should they buy a home?

a) Buy a home now and renegotiate the loan payment for five years.
b) Buy a home in a year after paying down the loan more than 60%.
c) Pay off the loan now and save for a 20% payment and then buy. *

Chapter Insights

Higher-Level Questions

- The single best way to improve assessments is to test above the remember level.
- We should assess important understandings and what people need to be able to do.
- A simple way to test beyond the remember level is to ask people to *use* what they remember within a multiple-choice question.
- Situation questions are often used to assess underlying knowledge and skills. To build good situations, we find relevant, realistic situations that require decisions and add relevant details and media.
- Many higher-level questions that align with what people do require distinguishing between best course of action and less-good courses of action. This means they must do the same in questions. Asking them to "select the best answer" is closest to what people do on the job.

Chapter References

Anderson, L. W. & Krathwohl, D. R. (Eds.). (2001). A taxonomy for learning, teaching, and assessing: A revision of bloom's taxonomy of educational objectives. New York: Longman.

Baker, E. L. (1971). The effects of manipulated item writing constraints on the homogeneity of test items. Journal of Educational Measurement, 8, 305-309.

Berk, R. A. (1996). A consumer's guide to multiple-choice item formats that measure complex cognitive outcomes. Pearson Assessment.

Bloom, B. S., Engelhart, M. D., Furst, E. J., Hill, W. H., & Krathwohl, D. R. (1956). Taxonomy of educational objectives: The classification of educational goals. Handbook I: Cognitive domain. New York: David McKay Company.

Christian M. R., Sergel, M. J., Mycyk, M. B., & Aks, S. E. (2017). Comparison of high-fidelity medical simulation to short answer written examination in the assessment of emergency medicine residents in medical toxicology. Missouri Medicine, 114(5), 396-399.

Clark, R. C. (2013). Scenario-based e-learning: Evidence-based guidelines for online workforce learning. San Francisco: Pfeiffer.

Cook, D. A., Hamstra, S. J., Brydges, R., Zendejas, B., Szostek, J. H., Wang, A. T., Erwin, P. J., & Hatala, R. (2013). Comparative effectiveness of instructional design features in simulation-based education: systematic review and meta-analysis. Medical Teacher, 35(1), 867-98.

Fazio, L. K., Agarwal, P. K., Marsh, E. J., & Roediger, H. L., III. (2010). Memorial consequences of multiple-choice testing on immediate and delayed tests. Memory & Cognition, 38, 407-418.

Gross, D. C., Pace D., Harmoon, S., and Tucker, W. (1999). Why fidelity? Proceedings of the Spring 1999 Simulation Interoperability Workshop.

Haladyna, T. M. (1997). Writing test items to evaluate higher order thinking skills. Needham Heights, MA: Allyn and Bacon.

Haladyna, T. M. (2004). Developing and validating multiple-choice test items. Mahwah, NJ: Lawrence Erlbaum Associates, Inc.

Haladyna, T. M. & Downing, S. M. (1989). A taxonomy of multiple-choice item-writing rules. Applied Measurement in Education, 1, 37–50.

Haladyna, T. M. & Downing, S. M. (1993). How many options is enough for a multiple-choice test item? Educational and Psychological Measurement, 999–1010.

Haladyna, T. M., Downing, S. M., Rodriguez, M. (2002.) A review of multiple-choice item-writing guidelines for classroom assessment. Applied Measurement in Education, 15, 309–34.

Haladyna, T. M. & Rodriguez, M. (2013). Developing and validating test items. New York: Routledge.

Haladyna, T. M., Rodriguez, M. C., & Stevens, C. (2019) Are multiple-choice items too fat? Applied Measurement in Education, 32:4, 350-364.

Kanjilal, U., Khare, P., Naidu, S., & Menon, M. (2014). Promoting scenario-based e-learning at IGNOU: Faculty experiences.

Norman, G., Dore, K., & Grierson, L. (2012). The minimal relationship between simulation fidelity and transfer of learning. Medical Education, 46(7), 636-47.

Schank, R., Fano, A., Bell, B., & Jona, M. (1993). The design of goal-based scenarios. Journal of the Learning Sciences, 3(4), 305-345.

Shrock, S. A. & Coscarelli, W. C. (2007). Criterion-referenced test development: Technical and legal guidelines for corporate training and certification (3rd ed.). Silver Spring: Pfeiffer.

Chapter 5:
Multiple-Choice Question Formats

R esearch finds some multiple-choice question formats work well, while others are problematic. Information in this chapter about whether to use these formats and when to use them comes primarily from Haladyna (1997), Haladyna et al. (2002), Shrock & Coscarelli (2007), and Haladyna & Rodriguez (2013). I'll discuss conventional, multiple-true-false, matching, multiple-correct, item sets, and complex formats in this chapter.

Conventional

The conventional format is recommended to use.

Conventional multiple-choice questions are the most common and widely accepted multiple-choice format. They include a stem with one correct answer (key) and two or more incorrect answers (distractors).

```
Stem
    a) Answer choice
    b) Answer choice
    c) Answer choice
```

There are two ways of writing the stem:
- **Question:** What does assessment reliability mean?
- **Incomplete sentence:** Assessment reliability means:

Some research shows that the incomplete sentence format is more difficult to understand because it requires readers to mentally combine the stem with each answer choice. Other research shows the two formats as equivalent.

There are two ways of answering conventional multiple-choice questions: Correct answer and best answer.

Correct Answer

With correct answer questions, there is one correct answer, and that answer is unambiguously correct. The other answer choices are unambiguously incorrect. For these questions, we ask test takers to "Select the correct answer." Here's an example of a conventional multiple-choice question with a correct answer.

Which part of a multiple-choice question presents the question or incomplete sentence? (Select the correct answer.)
   a)   Stem *
   b)   Key
   c)   Distractor

This question clearly has only one correct answer. The other answers are clearly incorrect.

Best Answer

With best answer questions, some answers may be partially or sometimes correct, but only one answer is best. People with the needed knowledge and skill should be able to distinguish the best answer from the other answers.

You may remember from Chapter 4 that there are important reasons we need to use best answer questions. There are stems where it would be difficult to say there is only one definitively correct answer because the answer depends on context. Here are two examples.
   • What is the best way to discuss tardiness with a staff member?
   • Should we control the amount of time off employees take?

The answer to both is likely, "It depends." If these were multiple-choice questions, we'd expect to offer context in the stem for selecting the best answer.

For best answer questions, we ask test takers to "Select the best answer."

Here's an example of a conventional multiple-choice question with a best answer.

What is the primary reason that distractors must be plausible? (Select the best answer.)
   a) Implausible distractors make the correct answer easier to guess. *
   b) Implausible distractors take extra time to read and understand.
   c) Plausible distractors distract attention from the correct answer.

Answer a is the primary reason we need distractors to be plausible. Answer c might be seen as true-ish but it isn't the primary reason distractors need to be plausible. Answer b, while plausible, is incorrect.

In questions with a best answer, the best answer is entirely correct. It isn't incorrect, partially correct, or sometimes correct. You might explain in the instructions what "select the best answer" means. Here's some example language to explain "Select the best answer."

The following questions have ONE BEST ANSWER. The other answers are either incorrect or are only partially or sometimes correct.

Multiple-True-False

This format is recommended to use.

Multiple-true-false questions include a stem and multiple answer options. Each answer choice is answered as true or false.

```
Stem
    a) Answer choice TF
    b) Answer choice TF
    c) Answer choice TF
    d) Answer choice TF
    e) Answer choice TF
    f) Answer choice TF
    g) Answer choice TF
```

Next are two examples of multiple-true-false multiple-choice questions.

Example 1

Examples of aseptic preparation used during operating room
procedures include: (Select True or False for each answer.)

a)	Disinfecting operating room equipment and instruments.	TF
b)	Not allowing ill workers to work in the aseptic field.	TF
c)	Disinfecting a patient's skin before making an incision.	TF
d)	Wearing sterile gloves and masks during procedures.	TF
e)	Limiting entry to the sterile field to necessary staff only.	TF
f)	Keeping sterilized instruments inside wrappers until use.	TF

Example 2

We implement food safety principles to prevent: (Select True
or False for each answer.)

a)	Incidence of food poisoning.	TF
b)	Bacterial growth in food.	TF
c)	Viral growth in food.	TF
d)	Serious intestinal problems.	TF
e)	Contamination of canned goods.	TF
f)	Contamination of dry goods.	TF
g)	Contamination of frozen foods.	TF

This question type is especially useful for assessing important
understandings. With a well-designed, multiple-true-false question we can
obtain insights into participant thinking. This can be especially helpful to fix
misconceptions and missing understandings. As a result, we should certainly
include misconceptions as distractors. (See Chapter 3 for more information on
using misconceptions as distractors.)

Research describes various scoring methods for multiple-true-false items,
differing primarily in whether they reward partial knowledge. In conventional
scoring, test takers are awarded points if all correct answers are chosen. In
partial knowledge scoring, test takers are awarded points for individual correct
answers.

Statistical analysis of different scoring methods is contradictory. It may be
worthwhile to award points for partial knowledge if it is valuable for participants

to have partial knowledge. For example, in the example question about aseptic preparation, it is critical to follow all aseptic procedures so we might not want to reward partial knowledge. In some questions, it may make sense to reward partial knowledge.

Matching

This format is recommended to use.

Matching questions offer two lists of related words or phrases. Test takers match the words or phrases in one list with the words or phrases in the other list.

```
Stem
A                B
 Item 1           Item 1
 Item 2           Item 2
 Item 3           Item 3
 Item 4           Item 4
```

Matching is a good format to assess whether test takers know the connections or relationships between the items in both lists. Some common connections assessed in matching questions include category/example, cause/effect, part/function, term/definition, etc.

Next is an example of a matching multiple-choice question.

Type in the recommendation (Column B) for using each question type (Column A). All the items in Column B will be matched once.

A	B
1. Conventional multiple-choice question _(b)_	a) Not recommended format
	b) Highly recommended format
2. True-false question _(c)_	c) Sometimes recommended
3. Complex multiple-choice question _(a)_	format

Matching is good to assess recall and understanding but typically not good to assess higher-level thinking.

To make matching questions easier to understand, we should use the following tactics.

- Provide clear and specific directions. Describe what is being matched, even when obvious.
- Describe how to record the answer. State whether the items will be matched once or more than once, and whether some items will not be matched.
- Order the items to be matched logically. Order items alphabetically, numerically, or chronologically when there is a natural order.
- Make any non-used items (distractors) plausible. Unused items should be plausible distractors and in the same category as correct answers.
- Keep items concise. Both lists should be as concise as possible.

Multiple-Correct

This format is sometimes recommended to use.

Multiple-choice researchers express concerns about asking participants to select multiple correct answers. This is because multiple-choice questions with more than one correct answer are more difficult and take more time to answer than conventional multiple-choice questions.

```
Stem
    a) Answer choice
    b) Answer choice
    c) Answer choice
    d) Answer choice
    e) Answer choice
```

Haladyna & Downing's (1989) multiple-choice question-writing guidelines suggest that we not use multiple-correct multiple-choice questions. More recently, Thayn (2010) reevaluated this position, as there are objectives we cannot easily assess with multiple-choice questions with a single correct answer. There are situations where participants need to select more than one correct answer to align with the actual task.

For example, consider the following learning objective:

Based on error codes, technicians will select the appropriate test(s) to correctly diagnose the malfunction.

To measure this objective with a single-answer question, we must focus on situations where there is only one correct test, which may not us allow us to assess this objective adequately. Here's an example of a question that assesses this objective and has multiple correct answers.

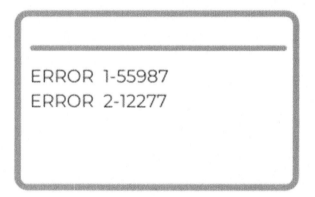

The BR220 is displaying these error codes. Based on what you see, which tests should you perform to appropriately diagnose the problem? (Select the two answers that apply.)

a) Monitor
b) Impedance
c) Line off
d) Forensics

Thayn's analysis helped me see that we can use some multiple-correct multiple-choice questions to assess objectives where we need multiple answers. These include objectives where people must be able to select multiple options, tools, situations, approaches, consequences, etc.

When we tell participants how many options to select, and the questions are clear, multiple-correct questions can perform well. These questions are usually more difficult and take more time to answer than conventional multiple-choice questions, so we should limit their use and use the following tactics.

Use multiple-correct questions when:
- Multiple answers are needed to achieve the learning objective.
- All correct answers are unambiguously correct.
- All incorrect answers are unambiguously incorrect. If any options are ambiguous (true in some circumstances but not others), then the question will be especially hard to answer. Use another question type.

Write them clearly.
Offer enough detail in the stem to make it easier to distinguish correct from incorrect answers.

Offer clear instructions.
- Tell participants how many answers to select. (Select the two…).
- On some testing systems we can set the correct number of answers. If test takers select the wrong number of answers, they will receive an error message. Good idea!

Don't trick people.
Use multiple-correct only when there is more than one correct answer.

The main reason to use multiple-correct multiple-choice questions is to assess an objective that requires multiple answers. Thayn (2010) explains that in these circumstances there is little or no advantage in participants having partial knowledge. If partially correct answers are inadequate to meet the objective, then we should consider not offering partial credit.

Thayn (2010) scored all his multiple-correct multiple-choice questions as correct or incorrect, with no partial credit. If there is significant value in partial knowledge, then applying partial credit might make sense (see Chapter 7).

True-False

This format is sometimes recommended to use.

True-false multiple-choice questions offer a statement and two answer choices: True/false, correct/incorrect, or yes/no. There is a lack of consensus regarding the use of this format.

```
Stem
    a. True
    b. False
```

Below is an example of a true-false multiple-choice question.

The D982 dishwasher has three heat levels.
```
    a)  True
    b)  False *
```

Shrock & Coscarelli (2007) say that using true-false questions makes sense for naturally binary (this/that, yes/no) choices, while it makes better sense to use other question types for non-binary choices. Although this format is widely used, some research points to problems (Grosse & Wright, 1985).

Item Sets

This format is recommended to use.

Item sets are situations with a series of multiple-choice questions.

```
Situation
Stem 1
    a) Answer choice
    b) Answer choice
    c) Answer choice

Stem 2
    a) Answer choice
    b) Answer choice
    c) Answer choice
```

Stem 3
```
    a) Answer choice
    b) Answer choice
    c) Answer choice
```

Below is an example of an item set and four multiple-choice stems.

John is a trainer for a case management organization. He is designing a new course on listening skills for case managers. The most important objective is the ability to listen effectively—especially during difficult, emotional conversations.

John is considering how he can obtain real-life discussions between case managers and family members to use in course exercises. Here are three of his ideas for obtaining real-life audio and video to use for these exercises.
1. Locate relevant recorded calls between family members and case managers and produce a series of audio clips.
2. Videotape in-person conversations between family members and case managers and produce a series of audio or video clips.
3. Record audio or video clips with staff portraying realistic and relevant discussions between family members and case managers.

Answer these four questions based on the details of this situation.
Q1: What is the most significant problem with idea 1? (Select the best answer.)
Q2: What is the most significant problem with idea 2? (Select the best answer.)
Q3: What is the most significant problem with idea 3? (Select the best answer.)
Q4: If John wanted to use one of these ideas, what should be his necessary next step? (Select the best answer.)

Item sets are especially valuable for more complex situations where several multiple-choice questions are needed to assess various aspects of the situation.

Try This!

Exercise 5-1. Choose the best multiple-choice format—conventional, multiple-correct, multiple-true-false, or matching— for each stem.

I completed the first item to show you how to do the exercise.

Exercise answers are at the end of this chapter. You will learn more if you do the exercise *before* you review the answers.

Stem	*Question format?*
Convection means:	Conventional A conventional multiple-choice question will work well for this purpose, as the question appears to ask for a single answer.
What is the primary reason mergers and acquisitions fail?	
Which of these will happen if you select the wrong option?	
What is the country of origin for each coin shown?	
Which of the following documents require signature notarization?	

Complex

This format is not recommended to use.

Research shows complex multiple-choice questions are problematic and should not be used (Haladyna, 1994; Case & Downing, 1989).

```
Stem

    1. Answer choice
    2. Answer choice
    3. Answer choice
    4. Answer choice

    a) 1 and 3
    b) 2 and 3
    c) 2 and 4
```

Here's an example of a complex multiple-choice question.

Which of the following medication classes were developed specifically to stop migraines?
   1. Anticonvulsants
   2. Anxiolytics
   3. CGRP inhibitors
   4. Triptans

   a) 1 and 2
   b) 2 and 3
   c) 3 and 4 *
   d) 1 and 4

To recap, the following table shows when to use the acceptable and sometimes acceptable formats.

Format	Best Use
Conventional	Default format when there's one correct or best answer
Multiple-true-false	Assessing related, important understandings; helps us diagnose misconceptions and missing understandings
Matching	Assessing related connections and relationships
Multiple-correct	Selecting more than one correct answer if needed to align with the actual task; use selectively
True-false	Naturally binary (this/that, yes/no) choices; some research points to problems with use
Item sets	Complex situations where several multiple-choice questions are needed to assess various aspects of the situation

Exercise Answers

Exercise 5-1. Choose the best multiple-choice format—conventional, multiple-correct, multiple-true-false, or matching—for each stem.

If your answers and mine don't match, consider why your answer might make sense before simply accepting my answer. We may have made different assumptions!

Stem	Question format?
Convection means:	Conventional A conventional multiple-choice question will work well for this purpose, as the question appears to ask for a single answer.
What is the primary reason mergers and acquisitions fail?	Conventional A conventional multiple-choice question will work well for this purpose, as the question appears to ask for a single answer.
Which of these will happen if you select the wrong option?	Multiple-correct, Conventional If selecting the wrong option leads to multiple problems, multiple-correct is a good option If selecting the wrong option leads to one problem, conventional may be the best option.
What is the country of origin for each coin shown?	Matching If the purpose of the question is to assess knowledge of connections between two items (country/coin in this case), matching is a good option.
Which of the following documents require signature notarization?	Multiple-true-false A multiple-true-false question format efficiently assesses whether the test taker knows which documents do and which do not require signature notarization.

Chapter Insights

Conventional
- The conventional multiple-choice format is a stem with one key and two or more distractors. There are two answer types in conventional multiple-choice questions: correct answer and best answer. This format is recommended.

Multiple-true-false
- The multiple-true-false question format includes a stem and multiple answer options marked as true or false. Research shows that the multiple-true-false format may be especially valuable for testing important understandings. This format is recommended.

Matching
- The matching multiple-choice question format requires matching the words or phrases in one list with the words or phrases in the other list. The best use for matching items is to assess the connections between the items in the two lists. This format is recommended.

Multiple-correct
- The multiple-correct multiple-choice format requires selecting multiple answers. Although it may be harder to understand and answer correctly, use this format when test takers need to select more than one correct answer to align with the actual task. This format is sometimes recommended.

True-False
- The true-false multiple-choice question offers a statement and two answer choices: true and false. There are arguments in favor of this format as well as arguments against. This format is sometimes recommended.

Item sets
- Item sets are complex situations with a series of multiple-choice questions. This format is recommended.

Chapter References

Berk, R. A. (1996). A consumer's guide to multiple-choice item formats that measure complex cognitive outcomes. Pearson Assessment.

Case, S. M. & Downing, S. M. (1989). Performance of various multiple-choice item types on medical specialty examinations: Types A, B, C, K, and X. Proceedings of the Twenty-Eighth Annual Conference on Research in Medical Education, pp. 167–172.

Dawson-Saunders, B., Nungester, R. J., & Downing, S. M. (1989). A comparison of single best answer multiple-choice items (A-type) and complex multiple-choice items (K-type). Proceedings of the Twenty-Eighth Annual Conference on Research in Medical Education, pp. 161–166.

Downing, S. M. (1992). True-false and alternate-choice item formats: A review of research. Educational Measurement: Issues and Practice, 11(3), 27–30.

Grosse, M. & Wright, B. D. (1985). Validity and reliability of true-false tests. Educational and Psychological Measurement, 45, 1–13.

Haladyna, T. M. (1992). The effectiveness of several multiple-choice formats. Applied Measurement in Education, 5, 73-88.

Haladyna, T. M. (1997). Writing test items to evaluate higher order thinking skills. Needham Heights, MA: Allyn and Bacon.

Haladyna, T. M., Downing, S. M., Rodriguez, M. (2002). A review of multiple-choice item-writing guidelines for classroom assessment. Applied Measurement in Education, 15, 309-34.

Haladyna, T. M. & Rodriguez, M. (2013). Developing and validating test items. New York: Routledge.

Shrock, S. A. & Coscarelli, W. C. (2007). Criterion-referenced test development: Technical and legal guidelines for corporate training and certification (3rd ed.). Silver Spring: Pfeiffer.

Thayn, K. S. (2010). An evaluation of multiple-choice test questions deliberately designed to include multiple correct answers. All Theses and Dissertations. 2450.

Chapter 6:
Feedback

Shute's *Focus on Formative Feedback* (2008) heavily influenced this chapter, and has been tremendously influential with researchers and others.

Instructional feedback includes responses by the instructor or the system about the test taker's answers. The right feedback can help correct participants' misunderstandings or missing understandings. Misunderstandings are often sticky, can damage learning and performance, and can be hard to correct later. Taken together, correcting them is a truly worthwhile goal.

In Chapter 1, I discussed how formative assessment typically offers feedback to designers, instructors, and participants to improve instruction while it's in progress (Black & Wiliam, 2007). Summative assessment evaluates achievement of the learning objectives—typically at the end of an instructional unit.

The primary goal of formative assessment feedback is to reduce misunderstandings and missing understandings. It typically informs participant and instructor next steps. The primary goal of summative assessment feedback is to tell participants how well they did. It typically occurs at the end of a module or course, often as grades or percentage correct. The primary goals of multiple-choice question feedback are to reinforce correct answers, correct incorrect and missing understandings, and help participants assume responsibility for the accuracy and completeness of their understanding.

Feedback is a complex and nuanced topic. It's impossible to offer instructions for giving feedback that works in most situations, so I've provided criteria for many of the tactics discussed.

Levels of Feedback

Research describes levels of feedback—from no feedback to feedback that offers additional information, such as an explanation of why the answer is correct or incorrect. The table below summarizes the levels.

Feedback Level		Description
None		No feedback given
Verification	KR=Knowledge of results	Whether submitted response is correct or incorrect
Answer	KCR=Knowledge of correct result	The full text of the correct response
Informational (Elaborative)	KCR+=Knowledge of correct result, plus additional information	The full text of the correct response, plus additional information such as: Why the answer is correct or incorrect Link to relevant instructional content Additional information such as: Hints Information about errors, misunderstandings, and faulty strategies

Timing of Feedback

The research on timing of feedback (immediate or delayed) is inconsistent. The primary purpose of feedback is to allow participants to correct errors and move forward. Kulik & Kulik's (1988) meta-analysis concluded that delayed feedback is superior in research settings, while immediate feedback is superior in real-life instructional settings. An explanation for this contradiction is that participants may not process delayed feedback in real life, whereas in research settings they are urged to do so.

Do Participants Read Feedback?

When we write feedback, we assume participants read it. However, research tells us this often isn't the case. Participants read and process feedback more often under certain conditions than others.

Research shows that participants read and process timely feedback more than delayed feedback. Although delayed feedback has benefits for long-term recall, feedback delayed too long may cause participants to lose interest. They read and process the correct answer more than other types of feedback. They are often unwilling to process long and complex explanations and are more interested in detailed feedback on higher-level questions. They tend to process and act on feedback on incorrect responses more than feedback on correct responses.

With delayed feedback they process only the grade. Participants who do well or poorly seem to make more use of feedback, while students who just passed make least use.

One reason participants engage less with summative feedback is that when they pass, they feel relieved and have achieved their goal. Under these conditions, they may feel unmotivated to address problems. Some research has successfully identified methods for motivating participants to read and act on summative feedback. For example, an instructor may add points to the score if participants explain the actions they intend to take based on feedback. This strategy has been shown to work with formative feedback as well.

Things TO DO

Research on feedback is conflicting, but here are some good ideas when providing feedback on multiple-choice questions.

Provide KCR feedback.

Feedback that shows the full text of the correct response (KCR) is more effective than feedback that tells whether the answer is correct or incorrect (KR). Participants read and process KCR feedback more frequently than informational feedback. As a result, I think we should offer KCR feedback for all questions.

Next are two questions from one of my course quizzes showing both KR and KCR feedback. Each question shows the selected answer choice (gray dot), whether the answer chosen is incorrect or correct (✗ or ✓), and the complete text of the correct answer (gray shading).

Well-written learning objectives are needed to write good
multiple-choice questions because:

- ○ They identify misconceptions participants have about the
  content.
- ● They describe what the content expert thinks participants
  need to know. ✗
- ○ They specifically describe the outcomes needed from
  instruction. Correct

How do we write good learning objectives?

- ● Needed job tasks and results tell us what participants
  need to be able to do. ✓
- ○ Stakeholders requesting training decide what needs to be
  learned.
- ○ Content experts writing test items decide what needs to
  be learned.

Provide feedback on incorrect and correct answers.

Pashler (2005) says feedback isn't needed on correct answers, but other
research shows there are benefits for feedback on correct answers—especially
for participants with less confidence about their answer. Giving the full text of
the correct response also improves recall of the correct answer.

Be concise and focused.

Keep informational feedback concise. Focus it directly on the question and
learning objective being tested. It's easy to overwhelm people who are new to
the content. Don't overwhelm them with too much information.

Consider when to provide feedback.

Provide feedback when participants can put it into action. Feedback should
influence the participant's next steps (re-read, redo, reconsider…). When
participants learn a task that is difficult compared to their existing knowledge
and skills, consider immediate feedback to prevent frustration and loss of
motivation (Clariana, 1990). When participants need feedback to proceed,
immediate feedback is beneficial.

Consider a delay between answering and receiving feedback. Although a lot
of research favors immediate feedback (Kulik & Kulik, 1988), the timing of
feedback is nuanced. We get better short-term gains from immediate feedback,

but delayed feedback has more benefits for long-term retention (Butler et al., 2007).

Delayed feedback may help people with more knowledge detect errors in their knowledge and review additional information while waiting for feedback. These extra activities can benefit retention and performance. But be careful about long delays—participants aren't motivated to read and act on feedback that is delayed too long. This is especially true for participants new to the content area.

Offer informational feedback for higher-level questions.

Participants are more likely to read and process informational feedback on higher-level questions versus recall questions. We discussed higher-level questions in Chapter 4.

Be conversational and constructive.

People read and relate more to writing that is polite and feels conversational than to formal writing. You should write as if you are talking directly to the participant and not as if you are talking to anyone.

Consider participants with different levels of prior knowledge.

The differences between participants with less and more expertise in the content being learned are significant. Shute (2008) supplies a list of differences between feedback needs for people with less and more knowledge.

For people with LESS expertise in the content area being taught:
- Offer immediate feedback.
- Offer structure, guidance, and support.
- Make feedback specific to the question and learning objective.

For people with MORE expertise in the content area being taught:
- Consider delayed feedback.
- Offer hints, clues, and prompts.

Consider using comments rather than grades.

Wiliam (2007) measured the effect of participants receiving comments, receiving grades, and receiving both. Receiving comments improved learning while receiving grades or grades plus comments didn't. The probable reason for this effect was that participants focused attention on grades in the latter two conditions.

Don't praise or discourage.

Don't offer feedback that praises or is likely to demotivate or discourage. Both are problematic.

Feedback for Computer-Based Instruction

Mason & Bruning (2001) reviewed research on feedback delivered during computer-based instruction and created a framework to help others include the right feedback. I adapted wording in their visual framework for ease of understanding.

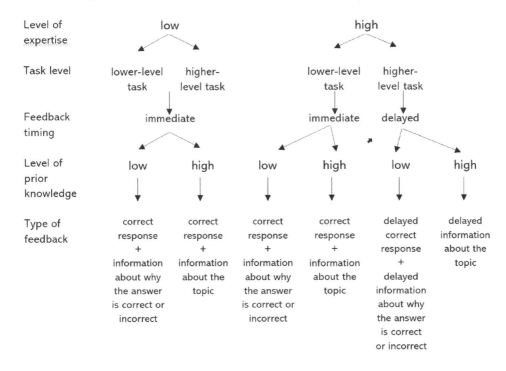

Adapted from: Mason, B. J. & Bruning, R. H. (2001). Providing feedback in computer-based instruction: What the research tells us. Research Report No. 9. Center for Instructional Innovation, University of Nebraska-Lincoln.

TRY THIS!

Exercise 6-1. For each assessment situation listed below, should we offer immediate or delayed feedback?

I completed the first item to show you how to do the exercise.

Exercise answers are at the end of this chapter. You will learn more if you do the exercise *before* you review the answers.

Situation	Immediate or delayed?
End-of-lesson quizzes in an online medical terminology course for people new to the topic	Probably immediate I assume the task is at a medium level of difficulty because of the amount of memorization needed. A low level of expertise and prior knowledge means immediate feedback is likely beneficial. Plus, immediate feedback can identify problems to be addressed before moving on.
Ongoing daily assessments for experienced networking engineers training as a team on new networking equipment	
Yearly, online, safe warehouse practices training for newer and more experienced warehouse workers	

Exercise 6-2. You train new hires in a small grocery store how to stock shelves and run the cash register. You developed many short quizzes, and new trainees take one or two each day. What is the most important feedback to provide after each quiz?

Exercise Answers

Exercise 6-1. For each assessment situation listed below, should we offer immediate or delayed feedback?

Situation	Immediate or delayed?
End-of-lesson quizzes in an online medical terminology course for people new to the topic	Probably immediate I assume the task is at a medium level of difficulty because of the amount of memorization needed. A low level of expertise and prior knowledge means immediate feedback is likely beneficial. Plus, immediate feedback can identify problems to be addressed before moving on.
Ongoing daily assessments for experienced networking engineers training as a team on new networking equipment	Probably delayed I assume the task is at a medium to higher level of difficulty. Experienced people learning complex new skills may benefit from a time delay to think through the issues. Idea: Give the assessment and then discuss the answers as a group the next day.
Yearly, online, safe warehouse practices training for newer and more experienced warehouse workers	Probably immediate I am assuming the task is at a low to medium level of difficulty and much of the training is a repeat for experienced people. Newer people may need immediate feedback. We may also want to offer immediate feedback so it is more likely to be read.

Exercise 6-2. You train the new hires in a small grocery store how to stock shelves and run the cash register. You developed many short quizzes, and new trainees take one or two each day. What is the most important feedback to provide after each quiz?

The full text of the correct answer
Why the correct answer is correct, why incorrect answers are incorrect
Fix misconceptions and errors in thinking

Chapter Insights

Feedback
- Instructional feedback includes responses to participant activities by the instructor or system. The right feedback can help correct participants' misunderstandings or missing understandings.
- The primary goals of multiple-choice question feedback are to reinforce correct answers, correct incorrect and missing understandings, and help participants assume responsibility for the accuracy and completeness of their understanding.

Levels of Feedback
- There are different levels of feedback, from no feedback to verification and from answer feedback to informational feedback. More feedback is not always better.

Timing of Feedback
- Although research shows benefits for delayed feedback, it is often impractical because participants are more interested in feedback when it's timely. It's often difficult to get participants to process delayed feedback. As a result, immediate feedback is often a better choice.

Do Participants Read Feedback?
- We assume participants read feedback, but this often may not be the case. Participants tend to read and process feedback that is on incorrect answers, timelier, targeted to the question, and not overwhelming or negative.

Things to DO, Things NOT to Do
- Participants with more prior knowledge in the tested content may benefit from hints and delayed feedback. People with less prior knowledge in the tested content benefit from more immediate and targeted feedback. We should offer what they need right now to continue.
- Research on feedback in computer-based instruction provides guidance on what feedback to offer in on-demand instruction.

Chapter References

Archer, J.C. (2010). State of the science in health professional education: Effective feedback. Medical Education, 44, 101-108.

Ashford, S. J. & Cummings, L. L. (1983). Feedback as an individual resource—Personal strategies of creating information. Organizational Behavior & Human Performance, 32, 370–398.

Azevedo, R. & Bernard, R. M. (1995). A meta-analysis of the effects of feedback in computer-based instruction. Journal of Educational Computing Research, 13(2), 111–127.

Bangert-Drowns, R. L., Kulik, C. C., Kulik, J. A., & Morgan, M. T. (1991). The instructional effect of feedback in test-like events. Review of Educational Research, 61(2), 213–238.

Butler, A. C., Karpicke, J. D., & Roediger, H. L. (2007). The effect of type and timing of feedback on learning from multiple-choice tests. Journal of Experimental Psychology, Applied, 13(4), 273–281.

Clariana, R. B. (1990). A comparison of answer-until-correct feedback and knowledge-of-correct-response feedback under two conditions of contextualization. Journal of Computer-Based Instruction, 17(4), 125–129.

Clariana, R. B. (1992). The effects of different feedback strategies using computer-administered multiple-choice questions as instruction. Proceedings of Selected Research and Development Presentations at the Convention of the Association for Educational Communications and Technology.

Clariana, R. B. (1999, February). Differential memory effects for immediate and delayed feedback: A delta rule explanation of feedback timing effects. Paper presented at the annual Association of Educational Communications and Technology convention, Houston, TX.

Cohen, V. B. (1985). A reexamination of feedback in computer-based instruction: Implications for instructional design. Educational Technology, 25(1), 33–37.

Corno, L. & Snow, R. E. (1986). Adapting teaching to individual differences among learners. In M. C. Wittrock (Ed.), Handbook of research on teaching (3rd ed., pp. 605–629). New York: Macmillan.

Dochy, F., Segers, M. S. R., Gijbels, D., & Struyven, K. (2007). Assessment engineering: breaking down barriers between teaching and learning, and assessment. In D. Boud, & N. Falchikov (Eds.), Rethinking assessment in higher education, 87-101. Routledge/Taylor & Francis Group.

Gaynor, P. (1981). The effect of feedback delay on retention of computer-based mathematical material. Journal of Computer-Based Instruction, 8(2), 28 – 34.

Guo, R., Palmer-Brown, D., Lee, S. W., & Cai, F. F. (2014). Intelligent diagnostic feedback for online multiple-choice questions. Artificial Intelligence Review, 42(3), 369-383.

Harrison, C. J., Könings, K. D., Schuwirth, L., Wass, V, van der Vleuten, C. (2015). Barriers to the uptake and use of feedback in the context of summative assessment. Advances in Health Sciences Education, 20(1), 229-245.

Harrison, C. J., Könings, K. D., Molyneux, A., Schuwirth, L., Wass, V. & van der Vleuten, C. P. M. (2013). Web-based feedback after summative assessment: how do students engage? Medical Education, 47, 734-744.

Hattie, J. & Gan, M. (2011). Instruction based on feedback. In R. Mayer & P. Alexander (Eds.), Handbook of research on learning and instruction, 249-271. New York: Routledge.

Hattie, J. & Timperley, H. (2007). The power of feedback. Review of Educational Research, 77(1), 81-112.

Hays, M. J., Kornell, N., & Bjork, R. A. (2010). Costs and benefits of feedback during learning. Psychonomic Bulletin and Review, 17, 797-801.

Kang, S. H. K., McDermott, K. B., & Roediger, H. L., III. (2007). Test format and corrective feedback modulate the effect of testing on long-term retention. European Journal of Cognitive Psychology, 19, 528-558.

Kluger, A. N. & DeNisi, A. (1996). The effects of feedback interventions on performance; A historical review, a meta-analysis and a preliminary feedback intervention theory. Psychological Bulletin, 119, 254-284.

Kulhavy, R. W. (1977). Feedback in written instruction. Review of Educational Research, 47, 211–232.

Kulhavy, R. W. & Anderson, R. C. (1972). Delay-retention effect with multiple-choice tests. Journal of Educational Psychology, 63(5), 505–512.

Kulhavy, R. W. & Stock, W. (1989). Feedback in written instruction: The place of response certitude. Educational Psychology Review, 1(4), 279–308.

Kulik, J. A. & Kulik, C. C. (1988). Timing of feedback and verbal learning. Review of Educational Research, 58(1), 79 – 97.

Lefevre, D. & Cox, B. (2017). Delayed instructional feedback may be more effective, but is this contrary to learners' preferences. British Journal of Educational Technology, 48(6), 1357-1367.

Lefevre, D. & Cox, B. (2016). Feedback in technology-based instruction: Learner preferences. British Journal of Educational Technology, 47(2), 248-256.

Marsh, E. J., Lozito, J. P., Umanath, S., Bjork, E. L., & Bjork, R. A. (2012) Using verification feedback to correct errors made on a multiple-choice test. Memory, 20(6), 645-653.

Mayer, R.E. & Moreno, R. (2002). Aids to computer-based multimedia learning. Learning and Instruction, 12(1), 107-119.

Mason, B. J. & Bruning, R. H. (2001). Providing feedback in computer-based instruction: What the research tells us. Research Report No. 9. Center for Instructional Innovation, University of Nebraska-Lincoln.

Merrill, J. (1987). Levels of questioning and forms of feedback: Instructional factors in courseware design. Journal of Computer-Based Instruction, 14(1), 18 – 22.

Moreno, R. (2004). Decreasing cognitive load for novice students: Effects of explanatory versus corrective feedback in discovery-based multimedia. Instructional Science, 32, 99–113.

Mory, E. H. (1992). The use of informational feedback in instruction: Implications for future research. Educational Technology Research and Development, 40(3), 5 – 20.

Mory, E. (2004). Feedback research revisited. In Jonassen, D. (Ed.), Handbook of Research on Educational Communications, 745–784. Mahway, NJ: Lawrence Erlbaum Associates Publishers.

Narciss, S. (2008). Feedback strategies for interactive learning tasks. In J.M. Spector, M.D. Merrill, J.J.G. van Merriënboer, & M.P. Driscoll (Eds.), Handbook of Research on Educational Communications and Technology (3rd ed.), pp. 125-144. Mahaw, NJ: Lawrence Erlbaum Associates.

Narciss, S. (2012). Feedback in instructional contexts. In N. Seel (Ed.), Encyclopedia of the Learning Sciences, Volume F(6), pp. 1285-1289. New York: Springer Science & Business Media.

Narciss, S. & Huth, K. (2004). How to design informative tutoring feedback for multi-media learning. In H. M. Niegemann, D. Leutner & R. Brünken (Eds.), Instructional design for multimedia learning, 181-195. Münster: Waxmann.

Nicol, D., & Macfarlane-Dick, D. (2006). Formative assessment and self-regulated learning: A model and seven principles of good feedback practice. Studies in Higher Education, 31, 199–218.

Pashler, H., Cepeda, N. J., Wixted, J. T., & Rohrer, D. (2005). When does feedback facilitate learning of words? Journal of Experimental Psychology: Learning, Memory, and Cognition, 31(1), 3–8.

Phye, G. D. & Bender, T. (1989). Feedback complexity and practice: Response pattern analysis in retention and transfer. Contemporary Educational Psychology, 14, 97-110.

Shute, V. (2008). Focus on formative feedback. Review of Educational Research, 78, 153-89.

Sinclair, H. K. & Cleland, J. A. (2007). Undergraduate medical students: Who seeks formative feedback? Medical Education, 41, 580-582.

Watling, C., Driessen, E., van der Vleuten, C. P. M., Vanstone, M., & Lingard, L. (2013). Beyond individualism: professional culture and its influence on feedback. Medical Education, 47, 585-594.

Wiliam, D. (2007). Keeping learning on track: formative assessment and the regulation of learning. In F. K. Lester, Jr. (Ed.), Second handbook of mathematics teaching and learning. Greenwich, CT: Information Age Publishing.

Chapter 7:
Scoring and Test Quality

Results of scoring research are mixed and confusing. Currently, research doesn't offer a best scoring solution. Experts suggest we score consistently and have a well-reasoned and documented scoring strategy (see Assessment Review, this Chapter). Many suggest using conventional scoring, even though it is far from perfect. Test takers understand it and we can write assessment instructions that test takers readily understand (Abu-Sayf, 1979).

Guessing and Answer Clues

"Guessing" is a general term that means the test taker has answered the question but is uncertain about the correct answer. Abu-Sayf (1979) says participants often use one or more of these guessing strategies.

- Select an answer based on "clues" such as the length of the answer choice, grammar clues, or clues elsewhere in the assessment.
- Use partial knowledge or misconceptions to eliminate one or more choices and choose from among the remaining answer choices.
- Find an answer choice that seems correct but with low confidence that it is the correct answer.
- Randomly guess among all choices, either by reading the options and guessing or by simply picking an answer.

Guessing is commonplace in multiple-choice assessments because many test takers have some knowledge to help them guess, and there is often no penalty for guessing. As a result, it is typically worthwhile for test takers to guess because they can eliminate incorrect answer choices. Research shows that guessing typically increases scores (Lau, 2011).

Here's a major problem with guessing:

Test score = what is known + what is correctly guessed.

The "real score" (what an individual test taker actually knows) is unknown to us. When participants don't know the answer, they typically try to eliminate answer choices, then analyze the remaining answer choices to find what is most likely correct. There are clues participants can use to help them guess. The solution, of course, is to eliminate these clues.

Grammar Clues

Grammar clues occur when one or more distractors don't follow grammatically from the stem. When this occurs, participants know that answer choice is likely incorrect. Here's an example of a grammatical clue and how to fix it.

This question has a grammatical clue.
We call the point in the Earth's crust where magma reaches the surface of a volcano a:
   a) Vent. *
   b) Ash cloud. (grammatical clue)
   c) Crater.

In this question, the grammatical clue is removed.
We call the point in the Earth's crust where magma reaches the surface of a volcano a:
   a) Vent. *
   b) Chamber.
   c) Crater.

Length and Depth Clue

Question writers often include more detail in the correct answer—and additional detail often makes the answer longer than other answer choices. When one answer is more detailed and longer than others, participants know the answer is likely correct.

This question has a length and depth clue.

You are using your outdoor wood-burning ceramic fire pit. Which of the following should you do to reduce the chance that flying sparks will ignite other fires? (Select the best answer.)
   a) Burn softer rather than harder woods.
   b) Douse the fire with water to put it out.
   c) Make sure there aren't any combustible materials, such as dead vegetation, next to the fire pit. * (length and depth clue)

In this question, the length and depth clue is removed.

You are using your outdoor wood-burning ceramic fire pit. Which of the following should you do to reduce the chance that flying sparks will ignite other fires? (Select the best answer.)
   a) Burn softer rather than harder woods.
   b) Douse the fire with water to put it out.
   c) Remove nearby flammable materials. *

Repeated Words Clue

When we repeat words or phrases from the stem in the answer choices, participants know the answer with the repeated word(s) or phrase(s) is likely correct.

This question has a repeated words clue.
Fluoroscopy means examination using:
   a. A fluoroscope. (repeated word clue)
   b. Computed tomography.
   c. An arthrogram.

In this question, the repeated words clue is removed.
   Fluoroscopy means examination using:
   a) A continuous X-ray. *
   b) Computed tomography.
   c) An arthrogram.

Scoring

This section discusses different scoring methods and issues with scoring multiple-choice questions.

Conventional Scoring

The conventional method for scoring multiple-choice questions gives points for correct answers and no points for incorrect answers or skipped questions. The score for the assessment is the sum of scores for all questions.

This table shows quiz results of a 10-question quiz scored using the conventional method. The total score is equal to the sum of all the points.

Question	Correct/Incorrect/ Skipped	Points Awarded
Q1	C	1
Q2	C	1
Q3	C	1
Q4	I	0
Q5	S	0
Q6	C	1
Q7	C	1
Q8	C	1
Q9	C	1
Q10	I	0
Total score		7

Conventional multiple-choice questions with common misconceptions as distractors offer insights into participant misconceptions. For example, consider the following multiple-choice question about the cause of seasons on Earth.

Seasons on Earth are caused by:
   a) Changes in the distance from the Earth to the sun at different times of the year.
   b) Changes in the Earth's axis changing the degree of tilt at different times of the year.
   c) Changes in the angle at which sunlight hits the Earth at different times of the year. *

The answer choices are the correct answer c and common misunderstandings a and b. By figuring out the percentage of test takers who chose answer choices a or b, we can analyze the approximate percentage of test takers with misconceptions. It is approximate because some people who chose answer choices a, b, and c did so because they were guessing—with or without partial knowledge.

Negative Scoring

Negative scoring was developed to discourage guessing. This table shows quiz results for the same 10-question quiz as scored using negative scoring. To get a total score, points are added for each correct answer and points are subtracted for each incorrect answer. Skipped answers receive no points. The total score is equal to the sum of all the points.

Question	Correct/Incorrect/ Skipped	Points Awarded
Q1	C	1
Q2	C	1
Q3	C	1
Q4	I	- 0.25
Q5	S	0
Q6	C	1
Q7	C	1
Q8	C	1
Q9	C	1
Q10	I	- 0.25
Total points		6.50

Research shows negative scoring often doesn't discourage guessing—especially when test takers have partial knowledge. Negative scoring may harm risk-adverse participants and benefit those with greater tolerance for risk.

Partial Knowledge Scoring

There is a large difference between random guessing and guessing using partial knowledge. Conventional scoring and negative scoring, though, offer few insights about partial knowledge.

Researchers (such as Bush, 2001) discuss the need to be able to analyze participant partial knowledge. This would provide a more complete understanding of participant thinking than is offered with most multiple-choice assessment results.

Here's an example of a multiple-choice question format useful for testing partial knowledge.

Circumnavigation in communication means:
   a) Being forceful and insistent that you are right.
   b) Responding to questions with more questions.
   c) Asking for time to think during discussions.
   d) Avoiding dealing with problems and difficulties. *

The correct answer is:

| A | B | C | D |

The correct answer can be:

| A | B | C | D |

The correct answer cannot be:

| A | B | C | D |

Lesage (2013) compares these three scoring methods (adapted for ease of understanding).

Issue	Conventional Scoring	Negative Scoring	Partial Credit Scoring
Scoring	Rewards correct answer No penalties for incorrect or skipped answers	Rewards correct answer Penalties for incorrect answers but not for skipped answers	Rewards full and partial knowledge
Partial Knowledge	Not considered	Not considered	Considered except when participant guesses the answer
Maximizing the score	Answer every question, guess	If you can eliminate at least one answer choice, guess	If you can eliminate at least one answer choice, guess
Problems	Encourages and rewards guessing	Doesn't discourage guessing, instructions may be confusing *	Doesn't discourage guessing, complex scoring

Adapter from Lesage, E., Valcke, M., & Sabbe, E. (2013). Scoring methods for multiple choice assessment in higher education: Is it still a matter of number right scoring or negative marking? Studies in Educational Evaluation, 39(3), 188-193.

* The Assessment Instructions section of this chapter explains that we should tell participants how to maximize their score. Negative scoring subtracts points for wrong answers while instructions tell participants that, if they can eliminate one or more answers, guessing is likely to increase their score. This is likely to be confusing.

Passing Score

The score we set as the passing score is the lowest score on an assessment considered passing. Some assessments have multiple passing scores that represent tiered levels of proficiency, such as "mastery," "proficient," and "starting."

I explained earlier that well-written assessments can be a proxy for directly observing people doing the job over time. Passing scores are meant to be informed judgments about the relationship between score and proficiency.

Although many people simply choose a passing score, this practice is problematic. Since the passing score is the lowest score at which we consider the test taker proficient, we need to think carefully when setting it. The performance standard (the learning objective) and the passing score must be in alignment as they represent the same thing (Kane, 1994; Cizek, 2005).

To consider the importance of the passing score, first analyze the consequences of sorting people into the incorrect proficiency level. This might mean proficient performers are considered nonproficient (they fail while proficient) and nonproficient performers are deemed proficient (they pass while not proficient). If the consequences are problematic, you will want to think deeply about setting a passing score.

The most common way to set a passing score is to analyze what is the lowest level of acceptable performance. Some ask proficient performers and content experts what percentage of minimally competent test takers should get each item correct, then calculate the mean from their answers. This adds rigor to the process.

An even more defensible way to set passing scores is to gather information over time about the assessment, including correlation between the assessment and performance. We can then adjust passing scores over time, so they best predict performance. For example, if you offer an assessment to sales reps on the sales process, you can compare their results on the assessment with their results in the field.

Impara & Plake's (2000) discussion of passing scores supports others' recommendations to use multiple methods to minimize potential bias, confirm results, and increase confidence that passing scores are properly set.

If you write high-stakes assessments, you may need to validate assessments and go further to set responsible and defensible passing scores. Some people do not test well but do well on the job or in other real-world settings. It makes sense, then, to consider alternatives besides assessments, such as supervisor and customer evaluations, and work products and results.

MORE...

Impara and Plake's article is available online—and I recommend reading it.

Impara, J. C. & Plake, B. S. (2000). A comparison of cut scores using multiple standard setting methods. Paper presented at the 81st annual meeting of the American Educational Research Association, New Orleans, LA.

To maintain the URLs more easily for online resources, they are available here: https://www.pattishank.com/mcqresources

Assessment Instructions

Assessment instructions are critically important, and they must align with the scoring method (Abu-Sayf, 1979). When stakes for tests are high, it's essential that instructions inform test takers about the strategy to follow to maximize their score.

He cautions us, though, that not all test takers can or will analyze how to best maximize their score given the scoring method. If we don't tell test takers how to maximize their score, we can expect measurement error and bias toward people who can and do perform the analysis.

Experts conclude, therefore, that we should provide test takers with the scoring method and the recommended strategy to maximize their score based on this method. Even if we tell them, risk-adverse and risk-tolerant test takers may operate as usual. The risk-adverse would omit unknown answers and the risk-tolerant would answer all questions.

There are other elements that may be worthwhile to include in assessment instructions, depending on the assessment.

Purpose of the Assessment
List the learning objectives the assessment covers.

Length of the Assessment
List the number of questions included in the assessment.

Time
Describe the amount of time the assessment is likely to take. If there is a time limit, describe how much time the assessment should take and what happens when the allotted time ends.

Navigation
Describe how to begin, proceed, navigate, and finish the assessment.

Feedback
Explain whether the system offers feedback, what is included in feedback, and when feedback is offered (after each question, after the assessment is completed).

Attempts
Describe how many times you can take the assessment and which score will "count."

Weighting
Explain whether questions are weighted and the impact of weighting on the final score.

Scoring
Describe the scoring methods and specific strategies to maximize the score, including guessing and use of partial knowledge.

Cheating
Describe the methods used to monitor cheating.

Assessment instructions must be as concise as they can be so people read them.

Example Assessment Instructions

There are [#] questions on this test. Each question is worth [#] points for a total of [#] possible points. The assessment is worth [%] of the grade for this [module, course]. You have [amount of time] to complete the assessment once you click START, but the assessment should only take [amount of time].

The test application presents one question at a time. When you click SUBMIT for each answer, the next question will appear. You can use the menu at the top of the screen to review or change answers. When you have completed the assessment, click FINISHED. After you answer all questions and click FINISHED, you will receive feedback about the questions you answered correctly and incorrectly.

The best strategy to get the highest score is to answer all questions where you have confidence you know the correct answer. For the rest of the questions, answer all questions where you can eliminate one or more answer choices. Most people who guess improve their score, and there is no penalty for guessing.

If you have technical difficulties, contact [email, phone number, URL]. If you believe the assessment is not working properly, please contact [email].

You can review these instructions during the assessment by clicking .

Assessment Blueprint

The purpose of an assessment blueprint is to help you make good testing decisions and document your decisions in case your assessment is called into question. The blueprint is typically constructed after writing good learning objectives and before writing test items.

An assessment blueprint helps properly address every learning objective and ensure that every question assesses a learning objective. This helps avoid objectives that aren't well assessed and questions that don't assess any learning objectives. It also helps analyze whether the questions address the same levels of thinking required by the learning objective.

An assessment blueprint often lists:
- The purpose of the assessment.
- The content being tested (typically the learning objectives but may include content outlines and other information about the instruction).

- The priority/weighting of the learning objectives.
- Thought processes assessed for each learning objective.
- The number of questions per learning objective.
- Item formats to be used.
- Scoring methods.

When you create the items, add them to the assessment blueprint to document how you implemented the blueprint. Many assessment blueprints use a matrix like the example below.

Learning objective	Priority 1-5	Thinking level	Format	Thought process	Number of items	Total points
1 (Terminal)	5	Use	MC	Evaluate	5	5
1.1 (Enabling)	3	Use	MC	Predict	2	2
1.2 (Enabling)	2	Understand	MC	Define	1	1

Assessment Review

Allow time in the question writing process to thoroughly review and edit items and instructions. It is extremely difficult to adequately review your own items (Haladyna & Rodriguez, 2013). As a result, it is helpful to have competent item writers review each other's work. A good editor can copyedit questions but, since they typically aren't item writers, they will miss many problems. We should review and edit individual items all along the question writing process and then proofread again at the end. Researchers suggest the following areas to review.

Content Review

Make sure that items appropriately assess the most important learning objective knowledge and skills. When they don't, discard them and write better items.

I suggest that item writers first write stems and have these stems reviewed to analyze whether they assess central and critical learning objective knowledge and skills. This prevents writers from writing entire questions that are discarded.

A process that works well when I work with item writing teams is to first generate a series of question stems for each objective. Then the team collaboratively selects stems that best assess the important knowledge and skills in each objective; analyzes whether any important knowledge and skills are missing; and then creates additional stems as needed.

Guidelines Review

Review all items to make sure they adhere to accepted item-writing guidelines (consider using the LEARNING OBJECTIVES AND MULTIPLE-CHOICE QUESTIONS GUIDELINES job aid). When we find violations of item guidelines, we need to fix the item.

Writing Review

Review the instructions and items to look for problems with understandability, style, grammar, and spelling. Assess the readability of items and instructions and evaluate whether readability is two or more grade levels below that of the lowest test taker reading level. Lower reading levels help all people understand the assessment.

Answer Key Review

Confirm that the answer key for the assessment is correct and there aren't any distractors unintentionally marked as correct. This happens more than you would think and has happened to me.

When we write test items, we should document the correct answer, why the correct answer is correct, and why incorrect answers are incorrect. Documenting the correct answer will help with the answer key review. Documentation of why answers are correct or incorrect helps to write feedback and defend our choice of correct answer.

Test the Test

After the questions are written, test them before going live. We often assess questions with content experts first and then field test them with a sample of proficient performers.

When field testing with content experts and proficient performers, items should perform as expected and testers should have a high score. Field testing allows the assessment writer to identify unexpected problems with items and instructions. When field testing, I often find items that don't work as expected (often due to lack of clarity), so field testing is worth the effort!

Item Analysis

Once you have adequate assessment results, you can perform item analysis. This is typically performed using a testing application or a learning management system.

Item analysis means performing statistical analyses using the item (question) responses and scores. These statistical analyses offer information about the items rather than about the test takers. The goal is to find items with problems we may need to drop, fix, or replace.

We spend a lot of time designing good questions—and rightly so. Despite this, it's common for items with flaws to make it through writer and expert scrutiny. Item analysis helps us find these flaws so we can analyze them and see what we need to do.

The image below represents an assessment with 25 items—six of which look problematic. By analyzing and then improving or changing items with flaws, we improve the overall quality of the assessment, which can improve validity.

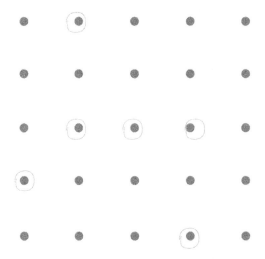

Finding out whether your testing system or LMS performs item analysis is tricky. If you ask whether your system does item analysis, you may be told that the application performs analytics. But item analysis is not the same as learning analytics. And item analysis may be called "item statistics" or "assessment statistics" or something else entirely.

Common Item Analysis Measures

Item analysis statistically analyzes the performance of individual test items. In this section, I'll discuss four common item measures:
- Response frequency
- Item difficulty
- Item discrimination
- Distractor analysis

Response Frequency

The response frequency for each item totals the number of test takers that selected each answer choice. Next are two examples. Each shows the multiple-choice question and the response frequency.

Clothing or equipment worn to protect workers from workplace hazards is called: (Select the correct answer.)
A. Personal protective equipment. *
B. Protective hazard equipment.
C. Workplace protective equipment.

Response frequency: A 41* B 5   C 4

When creating a workplace hazard assessment, which of the following should we do first? (Select the best answer.)
A. Send a survey to supervisors asking about hazards.
B. Do a facility walkthrough to find potential hazards. *
C. Do a focus group with staff to ask about hazards.

Response frequency: A 10   B 29* C 11

Item Difficulty

Item difficulty is how easy or hard the item is. It is the percentage of test takers who answered the item correctly. Item difficulty value ranges between 0.0 and 1.0 (0-100%). Higher values indicate the item is easier; lower values indicate the item is more difficult.

$$\text{Item difficulty} = \frac{\text{\# test takers who correctly answered the item}}{\text{\# test takers who answered the item}}$$

Response frequency: A 41*   B 5   C 4

$$\frac{41}{50} = 0.82$$

Here are common reasons that item difficulty value may be high/item is easy (×=more likely to be problematic, ✓= less likely to be problematic).

- × Participants knew the course content prior to instruction.
- × Items contain clues as to the correct answer.
- × Distractors are not plausible, making it easy to guess the correct answer.
- ✓ Instruction used a mastery learning approach.
- ✓ The learning objective is easy, so related items are easy.

Here are common reasons that item difficulty value may be low/item is difficult (×=more likely to be problematic, ✓ = less likely to be problematic):

- × Insufficient instruction.
- × Item is confusing or poorly worded.
- × Item has more than one correct answer.
- × The item is mis-keyed. (The wrong answer is marked correct.)
- ✓ The learning objective is difficult, so related items are difficult.

Item Discrimination

Item discrimination is a measure of how well an item distinguishes between those who know the content being assessed and those who don't. Since this is one of the primary goals of assessment, it's a key item measure!

An item's discrimination value ranges from -1.0 to +1.0.

- < 0 (negative numbers) indicates that people who answered the item correctly did poorly on the assessment. That's not what we expect to happen.
- 0 means the items did not distinguish between those who know the content being assessed from those who don't. We don't want this to happen.
- > 0 (positive numbers) indicates that people who answered the item correctly did well on the assessment. That's what we expect and want!

Typically, we analyze item discrimination values as follows.

Discrimination value	Typically means:
< 0	Negatively discriminating Those who answered the item correctly did poorly on the test. This is not what's expected, so there may be a problem, such as: • The item is poorly written. • The item is mis-keyed. (The wrong answer is marked correct.)
0	No discrimination We write items to discriminate, so this isn't what we want.
> 0–2.0	Low discrimination Low
> 0.2–0.4	Moderate discrimination Expected
> 0.4	High discrimination Not usually expected

These are the general steps for calculating item discrimination for a specific item.

1. Arrange test takers from the highest overall score to the lowest overall score.
2. Divide test takers into groups by score, including highest scores and lowest scores.
3. Count the number of test takers in the highest and lowest group who got the item correct.
4. Subtract the number of test takers in the lowest group who got the item correct from the number of test takers in the highest group who got the item correct.
5. Divide the result by the number of test takers in each group.

Let's look at two examples.

Example 1

#Correct
Highest 25
Lowest 10

Discrimination $\dfrac{25-10}{40} = 0.375$

Example 2

#Correct
Highest 12
Lowest 12

Discrimination $\dfrac{12-12}{40} = 0.0$

Example 1 shows an item that discriminates moderately well. Example 2, however, shows an item that doesn't discriminate.

Common reasons for a low discrimination value (×=more likely to be problematic, – may or may not be problematic):

- × Item is confusing, ambiguous, or poorly worded.
- × There is more than one correct answer.
- × The item is mis-keyed. (The wrong answer is marked correct.)
- × Item measures something other than what the assessment measures.
- – Item is very hard or very easy. (There are good reasons to have very hard and very easy items—especially when the learning objective is hard or easy.)

The most common reason for a negative discrimination value is that the item content is unrelated to the rest of the assessment. The correct answer may also be mis-keyed.

Distractor Analysis

Distractor analysis measures how well distractors function. We analyze the response frequency and expect to see:

A higher percentage of test takers choosing the correct answer than the incorrect answers. If this didn't occur, we need to analyze whether:

- One or more of the distractors isn't plausible.
- The correct answer is confusing, ambiguous, or poorly worded.
- The stem needs additional information to make the correct answer obvious.
- The often-chosen distractor is actually correct.
- The question is too hard.
- The information wasn't well taught.

A high percentage of test takers who don't have the needed knowledge selecting the distractors. If this didn't occur, we need to analyze whether:

- The distractors are plausible and well written.
- There are clues in the question about the correct answer.
- The question is too easy.
- Instruction used a mastery learning approach.

An acceptable value depends on the difficulty of the item. If we assume 0.7 is an acceptable item difficulty value for a specific item (70% of test takers got the item correct), we expect the remaining 0.3 (30%) to be somewhat evenly divided among the distractors.

Here's an example.

Response frequency: A 7   B 25*   C 8

More people chose the correct answer (25) than distractors (15). The difficulty of this question is 25/40 or 0.625 (62.5% of the test takers got the question correct). The rest is approximately equally divided between the two distractors. If, instead, 14 people chose answer a and 1 person chose answer c, we'd want to analyze whether there are clues to the correct answer and whether answer choice c is plausible.

When we work with small sample sizes, results may be due to chance. As more people take the assessment over time and we combine answer results, they tend to be more "normal." If your results seem off, you may be looking at too small a sample. Analyze for possible problems but analyze again when more people have taken the assessment.

TRY THIS!

Exercise 7-1. Using the response frequency shown in the last example, calculate the item difficulty.

Exercise answers are at the end of this chapter. You will learn more if you do the exercise *before* you review the answers.

Response frequency   A 7   B 25*   C 8

As a reminder, the formula for item difficulty is:

$$\text{Item difficulty} = \frac{\text{\# test takers who correctly answered the item}}{\text{\# test takers who answered the item}}$$

Item Analysis Indicates "Possible" Problems

An item analysis doesn't definitively find items that must be fixed, replaced, or removed. Rather, values suggest that we further analyze items that seem problematic. McGahee & Ball (2009) offer guidelines to analyze when a specific item may need revision. I adapted their guidelines below.

Highest Score Group	Lowest Score Group	Discrimination Value	Poor Distractors*	Action
correct	incorrect	positive	no	Do nothing
correct	incorrect	positive	yes	Revise poor distractors
incorrect	correct	negative	no	Revise test item
incorrect	correct	negative	yes	Revise test item and poor distractors
incorrect	incorrect	positive or negative	yes or no	Revise content/reteach

* Response frequency shows distractors rarely or never chosen

Adapted from McGahee, T. W. & Ball, J. (2009). How to read and really use an item analysis. Nurse Educator, 34, 166-171.

They recommend that item analysis not be the sole factor for revising assessment items. Item analysis offers clues, but we must also consider other information, such as the number of test takers (having fewer test takers typically means an unexpected result may be due to chance), differences in preparation, and so forth. For example, items with very high difficulty levels may indicate that the content wasn't effectively taught. Making the item less difficult will not solve the underlying problem.

Exercise Answers

Exercise 7-1. Using the response frequency, calculate the item difficulty.

Response frequency   A 7   B 25*   C 8

$$\frac{25}{40} = 0.625$$ This item is of moderate difficulty.

Chapter Insights

Guessing

- Guessing is commonplace in multiple-choice assessments because many test takers have some knowledge to help them guess, and there is often no penalty for guessing.
- Research shows that guessing typically increases scores.
- The biggest problem with guessing is that the "real score" (what an individual test taker actually knows) is unknown to us.
- We don't want to do anything that makes guessing easier.

Clues

- Participants make use of clues to help them guess. Common clues include grammar, length, and repeated words. The solution is to avoid clues in your question!
- Grammar clues occur when one or more of the answer choices don't follow grammatically from the stem. Length clues are when the correct answer is longer and has more details than the other answer choices. Repeated words clues are words or phrases from the stem repeated in the answers.

Scoring

- Guessing is problematic because part of the score is what people know and part is what they guessed.
- The most conventional method to score multiple-choice questions awards points for correct answers and no points for incorrect answers or skipped questions.
- Research compares scoring methods for multiple-choice assessments, and results are mixed.
- Currently, research doesn't offer us a best scoring solution. Experts suggest we score consistently and have a well-reasoned and documented scoring strategy.

Assessment Instructions

- Instructions are critically important, and they must align with the chosen scoring method. Testing instructions should include information about how we score the test and instructions for maximizing the score based on the test scoring method.

Item Analysis
- Item analysis means performing statistical analyses using question responses and scores.
- Item analysis doesn't definitively find items that must be fixed, replaced, or removed. Rather, the values suggest that the item may be problematic. It's our job to further analyze items that seem problematic.

Chapter References

Abu-Sayf, F. K. (1979). The scoring of multiple-choice tests: A closer look. Educational Technology, 19, 5–15.

Allan, S., McGhee, M., van Krieken, R. (2005). Using readability formulae for examination questions.

Baldiga, K. (2013). Gender differences in willingness to guess. Management Science 60(2), 434-448.

Bandalos, D. L. (2018). Methodology in the social sciences: Measurement theory and applications for the social sciences. Guilford Press.

Berk, R. A. (1996). A consumer's guide to multiple-choice item formats that measure complex cognitive outcomes. Pearson Assessment.

Betts, L. R., Elder, T. J., Hartley, J., & Trueman, M. (2009). Does correction for guessing reduce students' performance on multiple-choice examinations? Yes? No? Sometimes? Assessment & Evaluation in Higher Education, 34(1), 1–15.

Ben-Simon, A., Budescu, D. V., & Nevo, B. (1997). A comparative study of measures of partial knowledge in multiple-choice tests. Applied Psychological Measurement, 21(1), 65–88.

Bereby-Meyer, Y., Meyer, Y., & Flascher, O. M. (2002). Prospect theory analysis of guessing in multiple choice tests. Journal of Behavioral Decision Making, 15, 313–327.

Biddle, D. (2012). Adverse impact and test validation: A practitioner's handbook (3rd ed.). Scottsdale, AZ: Infinity Publishing.

Brassil, C. E. & Couch, B. A. (2019). Multiple-true-false questions reveal more thoroughly the complexity of student thinking than multiple-choice questions: A Bayesian item response model comparison. International Journal of STEM Education, 6.

Bush, M. (2001) A multiple choice test that rewards partial knowledge. Journal of Further and Higher Education, 25:2, 157-163.

Burton, R. F. (2004). Multiple choice and true/false tests: Reliability measures and some implications of negative marking. Assessment & Evaluation in Higher Education, 29(5), 585–595.

Case, S. M. & Downing, S. M. (1989). Performance of various multiple-choice item types on medical specialty examinations: Types A, B, C, K, and X. Proceedings of the Twenty-Eighth Annual Conference on Research in Medical Education, pp. 167–172.

Cizek, G. J. (2005). NCME instructional module on setting passing scores. Educational Measurement: Issues and Practice,15(2), 20 – 31.

Coombs, C. H., Milholland, J. E., & Womer, F. B. (1956). The assessment of partial knowledge. Educational and Psychological Measurement, 16: 13–37.

Dick, W. & Reiser, R.A. (1989). Planning effective instruction. Englewood Cliffs, NJ: Prentice Hall.

Espinosa, M. P., Gardeazabal, J. (2010). Optimal correction for guessing in multiple-choice tests. Journal of Mathematical Psychology, 54, 415–425.

Frary, R. B. (1989). Partial-credit scoring methods for multiple-choice tests. Applied Measurement in Education, 2(1), 79–96.

Guskey, T. & Pigott, T. (1988). Research on group-based mastery learning programs: A meta-analysis. Journal of Educational Research, 81(4), 197-216.

Haffejee, F. & Sommerville, T. (2014). Fairness in using negative marking for assessing true/false questions. The Independent Journal of Teaching and Learning. 9. 75-82.

Haladyna, T. M. (1997). Writing test items to evaluate higher order thinking skills. Needham Heights, MA: Allyn and Bacon.

Haladyna, T. M. (2004). Developing and validating multiple-choice test items. Mahwah, NJ: Lawrence Erlbaum Associates, Inc.

Haladyna, T. M. & Rodriguez, M. (2013). Developing and validating test items. New York: Routledge.

Holt, A. (2006). An analysis of negative marking in multiple-choice assessment. Proceedings of 19th Annual Conference of the National Advisory Committee on Computing Qualifications, 115-118.

Impara, J. C. & Plake, B. S. (2000). A comparison of cut scores using multiple standard setting methods. Paper presented at the 81st annual meeting of the American Educational Research Association, New Orleans, LA.

Kane, M. T. (1994). Validating the performance standards associated with passing scores. Review of Educational Research, 64, 425-461.

Karandikar, R. (2010). On multiple choice tests and negative marking. Current Science, 99(8), 1042-1045.

Kulik, C., Kulik, J., & Bangert-Drowns, R. (1990). Effectiveness of mastery learning programs: A meta-analysis. Review of Educational Research, 60(2), 265-299.

Kehoe, J. (1994) Basic item analysis for multiple-choice tests. Practical Assessment, Research, and Evaluation, 4(10).

Kurz, T. B. (1999). A review of scoring algorithms for multiple-choice tests. Paper presented at the annual meeting of the Southwest Educational Research Association, San Antonio, TX.

Lau. P. N. K., Lau, S. H., Hong, K. S., & Usop, H. (2011). Guessing, partial knowledge, and misconceptions in multiple-choice tests. Educational Technology & Society, 14 (4), 99–110.

Lesage, E., Valcke, M., & Sabbe, E. (2013). Scoring methods for multiple choice assessment in higher education: Is it still a matter of number right scoring or negative marking? Studies in Educational Evaluation, 39(3), 188-193.

Linn, R. L. (1994). The likely impact of performance standards as a function of uses: From rhetoric to sanctions. Paper presented at the Joint conference on Standard Setting for Large-Scale Assessments, Washington, DC.

Malau-Aduli, B. S. & Zimitat, C. (2012). Peer review improves the quality of MCQ examinations. Assessment & Evaluation in Higher Education, 37, 919–931.

McCowan R. J. & McCowan, S. C. (1999). Item-analysis for criterion-referenced tests. Research Foundation of the State University of New York.

McGahee, T. W. & Ball, J. (2009). How to read and really use an item analysis. Nurse Educator, 34, 166-171.

Morrison, S., Nibert, A., & Flick, J. (2006). Critical thinking and test item writing. Houston: Health Education Systems, Inc

Miller, P. W. & Erickson, H. E. (2001). Test Development: Guidelines, practical suggestions, and examples. Patrick Miller and Associates.

Mills, C. (1983). A comparison of three methods of establishing cut-off scores on criterion-referenced tests. Journal of Educational Measurement, 20(3), 283-292.

Nedeau-Cayo, R., Laughlin, D., Rus, L., & Hall, J. (2013). Assessment of item-writing flaws in multiple-choice questions. Journal for Nurses in Professional Development, 29, 52–57

Outtz, J. L. (Ed.). (2010). Adverse impact: Implications for organizational staffing and high stakes selection (2010). New York, NY: Taylor and Francis Group, LLC.

Prihoda, T. J., Pinckard, R. N., McMahan, C. A., & Jones, A. C. (2006). Correcting for guessing increases validity in multiple-choice examinations in an oral and maxillofacial pathology course. Journal of Dental Education, 70(4), 378 – 386.

Rush, B., Ranking, D. C., & White, B. J. (2016). The impact of item-writing flaws and item complexity on examination item difficulty. BMC Medical Education.

Shrock, S. A. & Coscarelli, W. C. (1998). Make the test match the job. Quality.

Shrock, S. A. & Coscarelli, W. C. (2007). Criterion-referenced test development: Technical and legal guidelines for corporate training and certification (3rd ed.). Silver Spring: Pfeiffer.

Schuwirth, L. W. T. & van der Vleuten, C. P. M. (2011). Programmatic assessment: From assessment of learning to assessment for learning. Medical Teacher, 33, 478–485.

Schuwirth, L. W., van der Vleuten, C. P., & Donkers, H. H. (1996). A closer look at cueing effects in multiple-choice questions. Medical Education. 30(1), 44-49.

Siri, A. & Freddano, M. (2011). The use of item analysis for the improvement of objective examinations. Procedia—Social and Behavioral Sciences, 29,188–197.

Vanderoost, J., Janssen, R., Eggermont, J., Callens, R., & De Laet, T. (2018). Elimination testing with adapted scoring reduces guessing and anxiety in multiple-choice assessments, but does not increase grade average in comparison with negative marking. PLoS One, 13(10).

Zieky, M. & Perie, M. (2006). A primer on setting cut scores on tests of educational achievement.

Where to Next?

I'd guess most people who read this book didn't start out thinking multiple-choice questions were this complex. Writing good multiple-choice questions is a skill. Keep practicing and you'll improve.

I'd like to give you some ideas on how to keep improving after reading the book. If you have a lot of work (and who doesn't?), don't worry about fixing all your past mistakes. Start using these skills with your current projects. Fix the most critical past assessments first and the others as you have time.

Look for opportunities to practice regularly. Refer to the book to remind you what to do and what not to do. It's easy to forget what to do if there is a lot of time between multiple-choice question writing sessions. So, consider helping and teaching others to sharpen your skills and remember what's most critical.

If you work with a team, ideally each person should read this book so they are on the same page. Team members can edit each other's learning objectives, questions, stems, and answer choices. Gathering everyone's input offers valuable insights and can also help question writers who are struggling.

To find research articles cited and listed at the end of each chapter, search by the title and author. You'll find a lot of them this way. If there's an article you can't easily find online, you may find it at a local research library, such as public university libraries. To be sure you can use their library, call and ask for their policy for using their computers and databases to find and download research articles.

The best way to get better and better is lots of practice. You may be interested in taking my *Write Better Multiple-Choice Questions* course. I describe it later and, if you reach out to me with your book purchase receipt, I'll gladly offer you a reader discount.

If you are ready to learn more, I recommend the following books.
- Haladyna's Writing Test Items to Evaluate Higher Order Thinking Skills
- Shrock and Coscarelli's Criterion-referenced test development: Technical and legal guidelines for corporate training and certification, 3rd edition

About Patti

Patti Shank, PhD, is an internationally known workplace learning expert, instructional designer, researcher, and author who is regularly listed as one of the most influential people in elearning and workplace learning.

Patti speaks at training and learning technology conferences and is the author of *Write and Organize for Deeper Learning, Practice and Feedback for Deeper Learning*, and *Manage Memory for Deeper Learning*. These books offer practical, evidence-informed tactics to improve learning outcomes. All of Patti's books are available on Amazon internationally.

Patti's primary areas of interest include instructional writing and comprehension, use of asynchronous and synchronous online technologies, building courses designed for skill building, formative assessment, and learning objectives that describe needed results and multiple-choice questions to assess whether the results were achieved.

She was an award-winning contributing editor for *Online Learning Magazine* and completed her Ph.D. at the University of Colorado, Denver. Her research on new online learners won an EDMEDIA best research paper award.

You can find Patti's more recent evidence-informed articles on eLearning Industry https://elearningindustry.com/members/patti-shank-phd. Sign up for her email list at the top of www.pattishank.com and follow her on Twitter: @pattishank.

Write Better Multiple-Choice Questions Course

This online course is available to start anytime and is available to individuals and teams. It includes self-paced content, many videos, extensive practice activities, multiple quizzes, and job aids. The course includes an asynchronous discussion forum to ask questions, read Patti's answers, and hear insights from others.

The course is specifically designed for workplace learning practitioners and adult learning instructors. Course participants say it helped them make significant improvements in their multiple-choice question writing skills. The course takes about 10 to 15 hours to complete.

If you send proof of purchase for this book to mcq@learningpeaks.com, you will receive a discount code for the course.

More information: bit.ly/bettermcqs.

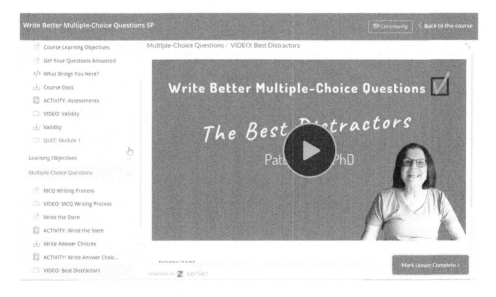

Index

Notes

Made in the USA
Coppell, TX
09 January 2023

10402207R00109